Contents

Contents

Staff and Educational Development Association

Equality, Diversity and Inclusivity: Curriculum Matters

Christine Talbot
University of Leeds

SEDA Special No.16
Advisory Editor Philip Frame
October 2004
ISBN 1-902435-28-1

Preface

The materials contained in the first edition of this workbook, 'Equal Opportunities and the Curriculum' 1999, were originally written for the Postgraduate Certificate in Learning and Teaching in Higher Education run in-house by the Staff and Departmental Development Unit at the University of Leeds. This updated version is once again intended primarily for those who are relatively new to teaching in Higher Education (HE), although it is also likely to be of interest to those who have been working in the field of higher education for some time but who wish to consider the issues of 'equality, diversity and inclusivity' in the curriculum in more depth than hitherto.

The book can be used by individuals working in a Higher Education Institution (HEI) or as the basis for group discussion of the issues, perhaps by those following some form of accredited course in teaching and learning in HE or participating in a short course on curriculum issues and equal opportunities. Hopefully it will provide a source of useful material that will provoke much thought and ultimately good practice, which will enhance your teaching and your students' learning.

The author is Learning Development Officer at the University of Leeds.
Email: **c.j.talbot@leeds.ac.uk**

Acknowledgements

I wish to acknowledge with thanks the permission granted by the author and W.W. Norton and Company, Inc. to reprint the quote by Adrienne Rich 1986, p. 199* (in the Introduction); by Oxford Brookes University Equal Opportunities and Diversity Coordinator Michelle Holliday to quote frequently from Janette Ryan 1997 'Equal Opportunities in the Curriculum: Good Practice Guide'; by Ian Law, University of Leeds, to use quotes from 'The Anti-racist HEI: a Toolkit'; and by Kym Fraser, University of Warwick, to quote from her forthcoming book, 'Educational Development in the Higher Education Sector'.

My thanks as well to Kate Heasman of NATFHE for providing me with NATFHE Equality Briefing on 'The European Directives', which is an invaluable summary of current legislation. There is not room to include it in this version of the guide, but it will be included in the fuller version of Section 2: The Context, available on application to me on the email address above.

I should also like to thank the many people from the November 2003 SEDA Conference who provided me with the stimulation and encouragement to finish the task of writing this revision, in particularly those who sent me the examples of good practice to include here, and Marion Bowl for permission to quote from her conference paper.

I am grateful to the two University of Leeds colleagues who reviewed the guide. They are Judith Russell, Head of the University of Leeds Equality Unit, and Joe Cortis, Chair of the School of Healthcare Studies Equal Opportunities Committee and Member of the University of Leeds Equality Committee.

(*Excerpt from "Invisibility in Academe", from BLOOD, BREAD AND POETRY: Selected Prose 1979-1985 by Adrienne Rich. Copyright © 1986 by Adrienne Rich. Used by permission of the author and W.W. Norton & Company, Inc.)

Introduction

'When those who have power to name and to socially construct reality choose not to see you or hear you, whether you are dark-skinned, old, disabled, female, or speak with a different accent or dialect than theirs, when someone with the authority of a teacher, say, describes the world and you are not in it, there is a moment of psychic disequilibrium, as if you looked into a mirror and saw nothing.'

(Adrienne Rich 1986, p. 199)

Why this guide?
In the late 20th and early 21st century, Higher Education (HE) has seen the welcome beginning of a shift away from a reactive, piecemeal approach to issues of equality, which were driven purely by a need to provide the bare minimum in order to comply with the law, towards a more pro-active, holistic approach to developing best practice in providing opportunities to improve the educational experience of all. Nevertheless, all such initiatives necessarily take place within the framework of legislation (much of it recently updated) that requires Higher Education Institutions (HEIs) to ensure that staff and students are not discriminated against on grounds of gender, racial group, disability, religion or belief, sexual orientation, and (from 2006) age .

One of the four main purposes for HE, as set out in the Dearing Report (NCIHE 1997) is to: 'to play a major role in shaping a democratic, civilised, inclusive society'. Various Government-backed initiatives, including the widening participation agenda, intended primarily to address the issue of inequality in educational attainment by those from the lower social classes, have encouraged developments in HEIs that have resulted in a much changed demographic analysis of both staff and students from that of a generation ago, and the emphasis of HE (in common with all other sectors of education) is gradually shifting towards the mainstreaming of issues of diversity and inclusivity.

However, whilst there have been a great many initiatives, and indeed progress, in the areas of staff recruitment and promotion and in the area of student admissions, particularly in the areas of gender and disability, less attention has been paid to the development of **a curriculum** that is wholly diverse and inclusive. Such a curriculum will make all students feel welcome and valued on all courses and (hopefully) help change attitudes of individuals and thus (in time) the broader culture of our society. As stated in 'Partnership for Equality: Action for Higher Education' (ECU and JNCHES, 2003), 'Education has a central role in developing the society of the future' (p. 7). This revised SEDA publication attempts to address these curriculum issues and to fill the gap that seems to exist in providing a basic introduction to this important area.

In the many years that I have been involved in the delivery and support of learning and teaching, it has always been clear that all teachers need to be creative. In the course of writing the original and now this version of this guide, it has become even more apparent that an inclusive curriculum is essentially an 'imaginative' curriculum. With a little forethought and a good deal of lateral thinking it should be possible to make the curriculum accessible to all. Hopefully this guide will provide the stimulus you need for creating a meaningful and imaginative curriculum for **your** students.

What's included?
The workbook is concerned with a detailed examination of how to create a diverse and inclusive curriculum. Based on educational research in the area of learning styles, approaches, needs and preferences, particularly in relation to age, gender, disability, as well as cultural, ethnic, and religious background, it looks in detail at ways in which those involved in teaching and learning in HE can influence the curriculum in order to ensure that no students are discriminated against in the process of learning and teaching and, further, that all students are positively affirmed as individuals in the course of their studies.

It includes practical guidelines based on good practice in the field, and there are ample opportunities to reflect upon your own attitudes and practices in this area.

It looks at all of this in the context of the current political and legislative climate in HE in the UK. It includes a comprehensive list of references and other resources, including many that are available online at no cost. Whilst there are a significant number of resources available with regard to how some areas of equality (especially disability) are impacting on the curriculum, other areas (such as religion or belief and sexual orientation) are still emergent and consequently a more limited amount of material is available.

What's not included?

This publication is not primarily about the employment situations of staff in HE, but rather how all staff in HEIs might influence for the better the curriculum offered by their institutions. The two areas are, however, inextricably inter-related.

Use of the materials

As has already been made clear by the use of the term 'workbook' the materials are intended to be used in the process of active learning, so you are encouraged to complete tasks from time to time and to make notes in a separate notebook or file, highlight those points which are, for you, key issues, and generally make the materials work for you.

There are also some points to 'consider' and respond to (and perhaps discuss with your peers), plus there are some specific examples of good practice included in Section 5.

If you are using these materials on your own, you may like to consider how you might measure the degree to which you have achieved the learning outcomes, perhaps by introducing an 'equal opportunities' perspective to student evaluation of the courses on which you teach, or by involving one of your colleagues in peer review of one or more of your modules.

Learning outcomes

It is expected that you will:

- be able to describe what is meant by an inclusive curriculum;
- be able to find information on Government and other initiatives that provide the context in which an inclusive curriculum is delivered;
- be able to identify specific aspects of the curriculum where equality and inclusivity issues need to be taken into account;
- have gone some way towards acquiring the necessary skills and knowledge to introduce measures to help ensure that none of your students is discriminated against as a result of the learning and/or teaching process.

Section 1:

The student body

1.1 What is a diverse and inclusive curriculum?

In the foreward to its guide on the 2003 Employment Equality Regulations, ECU (the Equality Challenge Unit) states: 'HEIs should endeavour to adopt a holistic approach to all equality and diversity areas to ensure effective mainstreaming and good institutional practice' (ECU 2003b, p. 2). Whilst the advice is stated within the context of staffing issues, it is good advice to all working within HE and with regard to all aspects of achieving 'equality, diversity and inclusivity' in our HEIs.

In considering curriculum matters, we need to move beyond the issue of simply encouraging a more diverse student body:

'Ensuring equal opportunities in the admissions process has no purpose if students do not have full access to the curriculum of the course they are studying.' (Skill 1997, p. 53)

An inclusive curriculum is one in which all staff and students feel valued, irrespective of age, gender, race, disability, sexual orientation, religious or personal beliefs, background or personal circumstances. It is also one to which all staff and students need to be committed. It requires effort on the part of all staff to ensure that such a curriculum is part of the student experience, whether studying with regular face to face contact with staff and peers on campus or via various media off-campus. It ranges from considering the practical issues that have to be addressed for a disabled student on fieldwork to ensuring that all learning materials provided to all students are non-biased, and it includes consideration of the best format and mode of delivery of those materials, especially for distance learners. However, we need to go beyond simply coping with diversity and practising inclusivity, in the face of an increasingly diverse student population and pressures to be more responsive to student needs, and move towards creating HEIs in which diversity is encouraged by positively promoting inclusivity.

'In a University the essential meaning of access must be "access to the curriculum".' (Borland and James 1999, p. 94)

1.2 Which groups of students?

Those working in HE have for many years been aware of the requirement to address the needs of students from 'overseas' or 'international' students within their institutions. However, in more recent years, the nature of the student body from within the UK has changed significantly. There has been a shift away from the traditional 18-year old, white, middle-class student (the majority of whom used to be male until recent years[i]) towards a more diverse student population, which more closely reflects the social make-up of society as a whole.

Such a shift towards an increasingly diverse HE system has been further encouraged by the publication of the Dearing Report (NCIHE 1997) and the subsequent government White Papers, 'The Future of Higher Education' (DfES 2003a) and 'Widening Participation in Higher Education' (DfES 2003b). Such diversity needs to be acknowledged in the teaching and learning which takes place within the institution, and measures taken to create a supportive, non-oppressive learning environment for all students.

Task 1

To begin to focus your mind on the issues which you are going to explore, make a note of those groups of people for whom higher education has not traditionally been easily accessible. Just spend a few minutes on this task then compare your suggestions with the list which follows, which itself is not exhaustive.

Commentary

You may have included some of the following groups:

- people from minority ethnic and/or religious groups
- disabled people
- mature entrants
- people without the traditional formal entry requirements
- people from a socio-economically disadvantaged background
- women who, although present in higher education institutions, are still very much in a minority on some courses
- lone parents, the vast majority of whom are women
- gay and lesbian students who, whilst having been present in the student population, have not (in general) had that presence acknowledged

1.3 How many students are we talking about?

The potential numbers of people in these groups is enormous. The Office for National Statistics in the 2001 Census and other reports provides us with a rich source of information about the population of the UK of around 59 million. HEIs can use this to identify the nature of the population they are seeking to attract into HE: 77 per cent of people in England and Wales are over 18; over half of the population of Great Britain is female[ii] ; although 87 per cent of the population of England and 96 per cent of the population of Wales gave their ethnic origin as White British, the proportion of people in minority ethnic groups in the UK rose to 8 per cent in 2001; and according to the Disability Rights Commission (DRC) there are 8.6 million disabled people in Britain – that's around one in seven (14.6 per cent). In the 2001 Census almost 77 per cent of the total population in the UK reported having a religion. It has been estimated that approximately 10 per cent of the population is gay or lesbian[iii] .

The Census also revealed that almost 30 per cent of households in England and Wales contain dependent children and one in nine have children under five. Just under one in ten households in England and Wales are lone-parent (9.6 per cent) and more than nine out of ten of these are headed by a woman. Two thirds of lone-parent households have dependent children.

According to the latest available figures from HESA (2002–03) there are over 1.5 million UK undergraduate and nearly 360,000 UK postgraduate students – in total nearly 1.9 million students – over 3 per cent of the total population. UCAS applicants are now requested to give information about age, gender, ethnicity and disability. Your HEI probably records this information for those students who successfully apply for a place on one of its courses. Similar information may also be recorded for non-UCAS students.

Task 2

Try to obtain statistical information (from the person who holds student records) about the students in your university, your department and in particular for one module/programme of study on which you teach. Have a look at how many students there are in particular groups, for example women, overseas students, disabled students and UK students from minority ethnic groups. [You may find that such figures are not easily available to you. If this is indeed the case, consider the implications of this.]

Commentary

Tables 1 and 2 (overleaf) contain the most up-to-date data available for all students at the University of Leeds (as an example) and students at all UK HEIs respectively.

Table One: University of Leeds - Student Statistics 2003/04
Percentages of students in particular categories

	Full-time students	Part-time students	All students
Disabled students - home (UK) only	5.2	5.8	5.3
Students from a minority ethnic group - home (UK) only	9.3	9.1	9.3
Male students - home and overseas	44.8	38.0	43.9
Female students - home and overseas	55.2	62.0	56.1
Undergraduate female students	55.8	71.0	57.0
Postgraduate (t&r) female students	52.1	54.9	53.1
Non EC overseas students (ug & pg)	11.3	15.8	12.0

Table Two: National Student Statistics 2002/03
Percentages of students in particular categories

	All students (ug & pg) as at 01 December 2002*	First year students (ug & pg) as at 01 December 2002*
Male students - home and overseas	43.4	41.9
Female students - home and overseas	56.6	58.1
Students from a minority ethnic group - UK domiciled only	14.5	14.7
Disabled students – UK domiciled only	4.9	4.3

* Figures published by the Higher Education Statistics Agency 2004

Task 3

How do the figures for your module/programme of study which you collected as part of Task 2 (if you were able to obtain them) compare with the figures for your university as a whole and with the figures in the National table above?

As the national table shows, women now represent more than half of all higher education students. They also represent the majority of part-time students (see figures for Leeds in Table 1 as an example). As reported in the Times Higher (Johnston 2004), a record 22,000 more women than men were offered places on full-time degree courses in the UK for 2003–04. There are also some major differences across subjects within institutions. Male participation is low in Education and in subjects and professions allied to Healthcare and Medicine, whereas there are relatively few women in subjects such as Science, Engineering, Technology and Computing.

There was a general increase in the number of students across all age groups accepted (1.7 per cent) but the most significant figure was the increase of 6.8 per cent among the over-25s. HEFCE reported in 2004 that the proportion of students in receipt of the disabled students' allowance (DSA) rose from 1.5 per cent in 2000 –01 to 2.1 per cent in 2001–02 (Sanders 2004).

1.4 What is your role in this?

Although the issue of equality of access to higher education is a very big and complex one which needs to be addressed by the Government and by the management of our HEIs, any individual member of staff who has contact with students or with potential students has a direct part to play in trying to ensure the creation of an environment in which every individual is valued, and where no-one is discriminated against. For example, the University of Leeds Equality and Diversity Policy states under the heading 'Responsibilities of individual members of the University':

In order to ensure that the Equality and Diversity Policy is put into practice, individual members of the University:

- should seek actively to promote equality of opportunity for others and strive to create an environment in which academic goals may be pursued without fear or intimidation;
- must not discriminate unfairly in the way they provide or procure services on behalf of the University;
- must not discriminate unfairly if involved in the recruitment, promotion and management of staff or in the selection and supervision of students;

- must not encourage other staff or students to practice unfair discrimination or harassment;
- must not victimise any person who has complained of harassment or unfair discrimination, or who has given information in connection with such a complaint.

Clearly these responsibilities are much more wide-ranging than simply the curriculum, but they serve as a reminder that all aspects of life of a university affect the overall culture of the institution. Further, since the introduction of a whole range of new UK laws to fulfil the requirements of recent European Directives, there is now a legal obligation on all staff to comply. However, alongside the consideration of the legislation, there has been a growing recognition of the moral responsibility of all HEIs to encourage those from all sectors of our diverse society to participate in HE, and further to actively promote in institutions positive relationships between all of its members. As Fraser (due October 2004) puts it:

'While complying with legislation is necessary there is also a moral component to be considered: it is morally right to engender an environment that includes all people, to recognize that "diversity is normal" and to create environments that are universally accessible.'

Endnotes

[i] Nationally, men constituted 58% of undergraduates and 63% of postgraduates as recently as 1985 (Holdsworth, 1988, p. 57). The split for all students was 60:40 male: female in 1985/56 and 66:34 in 1975/76, according to University Grants Committee statistics.

[ii] Office for National Statistics January 2004: 30.3 million (51 per cent) females compared with 28.9 million (49 per cent) males in mid-2002.

[iii] Although figures are not collected on sexual orientation and although many people do not 'come out', it has been estimated that approximately 10% of the population is gay or lesbian. It could therefore be assumed by all members of staff that there are likely to be some gay or lesbian students in any large group. Accurate figures for lesbians and gay men have proved to be difficult to collect. Figures vary from one study to another. Even within the same study by Kaye Wellings et al. *'Sexual behaviour in Britain: the national survey of sexual attitudes and lifestyles'* Penguin, 1994, the figures varied between those collected in face to face interviews and those provided in self-completion booklets. The figures from the latter indicated 6.1% of men and 3.4% of women reported some kind of homosexual experience.

Section 2:

The context

Since the publication of the first version of this SEDA guide in 1999 under the title 'Equal Opportunities and the Curriculum' there have been, I'm pleased to report, significant initiatives in the important area of equal opportunities in HE in the UK. [Due to the lack of space a very brief summary is provided here, though a comprehensive list of references and other resources **is** provided at the end of the publication. A fuller version of this section is available from the author on request. Please email – see Preface.]

The main emphasis (and some would say rightly so) has been upon equality of employment opportunity for staff employed in HE, especially with regard to meeting the requirements of new legislation with respect to race, religion or belief, sexual orientation, and disability, some of which will be referred to later in this guide.

However, other initiatives have placed greater attention on the recruitment and progress of students too. In particular, the Government's agenda outlined in the White Paper (DfES 2003) is to increase the number of 18–30 year old English students in higher education from the current 43 per cent to 50 per cent by the end of the decade, to increase the proportion of the whole labour force educated to degree level in the UK from the current 17 per cent, and to attract an extra 50,000 HE students to the UK from outside Europe by 2005. There has been a particular emphasis on 'widening participation' (WP) reinforced by the *Widening Participation in Higher Education* Report published in April 2003.

The widening participation aspirations of the above papers are reflected in the *HEFCE strategic plan 2003-08* (HEFCE 2003b) in which HEFCE's Mission was stated as: 'Working in partnership, we promote and fund high-quality, cost-effective teaching and research, **meeting the diverse needs of students**, the economy and society.' (Emphasis added).

In all of this WP is largely interpreted by the Government as attracting students from the lower social classes.

Some, however, are disappointed with this rather narrow interpretation and have a much broader agenda, emphasising the need to increase recruitment and address the needs of students from all non-traditional backgrounds (full and part-time), including disabled students, those from minority ethnic backgrounds, mature students, and men and women for whom some subjects have been non-traditional into those areas of study. Issues of race and disability in HEIs have been particularly dominant, since the implications of the legislation in these areas has extended to all areas of education, not just staffing. The independent disabled students' charity, *Skill,* has reported that disabled students are only half as likely to go to university as non-disabled students, and has called on the Government to widen the focus of the proposals it announced in the WP in HE Report for the Office for Fair Access, which made no mention of disabled students.

The authors of the anti-racist toolkit (Turney et al. 2002) also commented on the narrow remit of the widening participation agenda:

'The focus of WP has tended to be on particular groups defined by social class, however issues of "race", ethnicity, gender and disability (amongst others) should also be taken into account here.' (Turney et al. 2002, p. 79)

They stress the need for issues of retention and student support to be taken on board as well as student admissions:

'There is little point in getting students into an institution, only for them to find that there is inappropriate support and resources for their needs and which puts them in a position where they would rather leave than continue their studies and training.' (ibid)

One of the implications of the widening participation goal is that now, more than ever, HEIs need to ensure that the curriculum being offered is valid for a widening sector of society, not least so that the increasing numbers of students are fully engaged in what they are studying, are not alienated from their institutions, and that levels of attrition do not become unacceptably high.

Section 3:

How do we achieve equality, diversity and inclusivity in the curriculum?

As stated in the 'Introduction' to Oxford Brookes University's Equal Opportunities Action Group Report (Ryan 1997), 'equal opportunities' is not about sameness, nor is it about 'add-ons':

'The overall objective should be to ensure that diversity and equality are embedded in the planning, delivery and assessment of all teaching and learning ... . Equal opportunities is not about treating everyone the same. It is about recognising that people have different needs and that some people suffer greater levels of disadvantage and discrimination than others. In the curriculum, it is about positively responding to "diversity" and ensuring equality of opportunities in terms of access, treatment and outcomes.' (p. 5)

Marion Bowl (2003), at the SEDA Conference 'Values and changes in Higher Education' in 2003, posed the following questions, as prompts to identifying some of the ways in which we might respond to diversity:

'How can we ensure that the curriculum is organised in such a way that silenced voices are heard?'

'How can classroom discussion be organised to ensure that there is "safe space" for difference to be acknowledged and conflict faced?'

'How can we strike a balance between desire for objectivity and "evidence from respected sources" and the lived experience of students, who whilst they have much to learn, also have much to teach the traditional middle-class, white, affluent, child-free constituency of the university?'

Various delegates in the course of the conference, and since, shared ways in which they attempt to address diversity in their own institutions.

Some of those ways are offered in this guide, as suggestions to be adopted or adapted to your own particular subject and institution.

3.1 What is the curriculum?

Before looking in detail at practical ways in which the needs of a diverse student body can be met with regard to curriculum development, it is perhaps appropriate first to reflect upon what we mean by the word 'curriculum'.

At a conference entitled 'Equal Opportunities and the Curriculum' held at Oxford Brookes University back in 1997, great emphasis was placed upon the necessity to consider equal opportunity implications in every area of the curriculum. A very broad definition of the term was encouraged. This included all aspects of the process of education of students and ranged from issues of access to monitoring of outcomes, that is, attainment by students.

Task 4

In your notebook write down any areas which you think need to be considered under the broad definition of the word 'curriculum' when looking at equal opportunities issues. An understanding of curriculum is obviously crucial to this workbook, but it is suggested that you don't spend more than a few minutes on this task.

Commentary

You may have included some of the following:
- staff recruitment and student access
- course materials - subject content, language, case studies, visual images
- assessment
- modes of delivery
- attitudes/behaviour/comments of staff and students
- teaching/learning methods/styles
- student progression/drop out

- work placements
- field trips
- study skills
- student support - guidance, childcare facilities, language learning
- course organisation - timetables, timing of assessment
- student research[iv]

Healey, Jenkins, Leach and Roberts (GDN 2001a, p. 45), in the context of looking at issues related to disabled students participating in fieldwork, provide the following useful insight:

'For some the term "*curriculum*" just signifies content – *what* is to be studied. We take the curriculum at its widest, and we think most useful sense, to mean *the way that student learning is structured*. So this definition leads to concern not only with content, but also with teaching methods and assessment. It also directs our attention to what some call the "*hidden curriculum*", those subtle messages that staff and students send as to what is valued, for example that climbing high mountains in big boots and tee-shirts is a "good thing", or that exploration of alien cultures and landscapes overseas is inherently of greater value than careful analysis of local and perhaps more familiar and accessible settings. This wider view of the curriculum also directs us to consider the "*co-curriculum*", the wider student life and learning outside the formal curriculum – i.e. that students need to earn money may impact on their ability to engage with the fieldwork programme, and the informal curriculum of student behaviour on the fieldcourse, e.g. that evenings are typically spent in the bar. This wide view of the curriculum we believe is valuable to all teaching, but it is particularly pertinent to fieldwork for here the boundaries between the "*formal curriculum*" that is written down and the wider, but no less real, "*lived curriculum*" are clearly blurred.'

3.2 Meeting the needs of a diverse student body

All component parts of the curriculum need to encourage a deeper approach to learning than that sometimes taken by some students. Some learning traits are not fixed – they can be modified by the learning context, which you control.

Conversely, if learning preferences (which are more stable) can be matched to a large extent by the way learning tasks are set by teachers then the learning outcomes of students are going to improve. Although your teaching and the way you encourage students to learn cannot hope to fully incorporate the preferred learning styles of all of the students all of the time, it is nevertheless crucial to include a sufficiently varied approach to teaching and learning so that people in one or more of the constituent groups do not feel excluded or invisible all of the time either. (For a summary of learning styles, approaches and preferences see Appendix 1.)

In addition, all aspects of the curriculum need to be inclusive. As well as the obvious need to recruit more teachers who are women for some subjects (for example engineering) and more men for others (for example Healthcare Studies), or who are from minority ethnic backgrounds, or who are disabled, we need to closely examine a number of areas. These will include: the choice (including formats) of educational materials; the language used in the teaching/learning situation, both orally and in written form; teaching methods (all of which contribute to the content and delivery of learning and teaching); and the forms of and criteria for assessment. In all of these situations there is a danger that students who do not conform to the white, middle-class, able-bodied, heterosexual model will potentially feel unimportant, demeaned, ridiculed, or simply just ignored, and may actually be discriminated against. As stated by Susan Orr[v]: 'We need to acknowledge the partiality inherent in the curriculum'.

It is crucial that the environment in which teaching and learning takes place should be a positive one for all students. This is affected by many aspects of the curriculum, some of which are explored below. In all of this it is important not to regard diversity in the student body as a 'problem', but rather we should embrace that very diversity, using it to enrich the curriculum and thus the experience of ALL students.

[iv] This workbook does not deal specifically with research students. For a review of the issues relating to overseas research students see: Aboutorabi (1995).
[v] SEDA Conference November 2003

Section 4:

Content of the curriculum

Course content needs to be viewed from many different perspectives. The historical, cultural, political, and socio-economic perspectives from which subjects are viewed by students are generally determined by the staff.

4.1 Staffing

Clearly some subjects need to change significantly if a diverse student body is to be attracted to them. Not only are women students under-represented in several subject areas (predominantly science and engineering) but so are students from minority ethnic groups. In some subjects there is a self-perpetuation of the situation. For example, if there is a lack of women tutors or support staff, or of tutors or other staff from a variety of ethnic groups, there are no positive role models for students from these groups. White males attract more white males. Consequently content in some subject areas is skewed to areas more likely to be of interest to white men and thus less likely to attract women, or students from other ethnic groups. One point at which this cycle could be broken would appear to be at the staff recruitment stage. However there have been reports of women who have a tough time joining a predominantly male staff. Nothing short of a change in the 'culture' of the subject will actually bring about change in staff and student recruitment to these areas. Hopefully, initiatives such as the 'Athena' Projects and 'AWiSE' will gradually improve things in the areas of science, engineering and technology (see References and Resources).

There is a potential conflict for overseas students with regard to staffing. Although the status of the teacher is much higher in some countries than in the UK, the status of women is not in some instances. This can create tensions for male students who are taught by female staff.

One female academic who is interviewed in the UKCOSA (1994) video has found that she can overcome this problem and comments: ' ... somebody like myself presents themselves in the role of teacher and not through the gender issue'. The degree to which male students can accept the female teacher in her role as teacher rather than as a woman is variable.

4.2 Learning materials

One very important starting point for bringing about such a culture change is in the choice of course materials used. Materials which have positive images of women or Black and minority ethnic (BME)[vi] or disabled people will validate women or Black and minority ethnic or disabled students in their choice of subject. They will also give positive messages about people in these groups to ALL students. Research has found that diversity in the curriculum can encourage greater participation by, for example, overseas students, if it is demonstrated that their backgrounds and experiences are valued. This in turn improves their self-esteem and confidence (Ryan 1997, p.26). This, of course, applies to all students.

The 'images' referred to may not actually be graphical ones, though clearly any pictorial representation needs to be positive and non-stereotypical. Powerful images are portrayed through the written word, especially in the study of, for example, literature. Similarly, any case studies used in learning and assessment need to include women and men, as well as people from minority ethnic groups, people from various religions, of different ages and sexual orientation. It is especially important in some subject areas that are heavily gendered that there are role models presented in the course materials from both sexes.

For example, arts subjects attract more women than men, therefore it is important to have male role models, whereas the opposite is true in, say, engineering, where there are relatively few women students. It is also crucial to avoid Eurocentrism by using materials which present a variety of social, political, economic and spiritual perspectives. Eurocentrism assumes the superiority of the European culture to the detriment of other cultures. (For a fuller definition see Hall 1992 and Swartz 1992, p. 35.) It is all too easy to use culturally specific examples to describe, say, processes. For example, setting out the stages of making and serving a cup of tea from a UK perspective won't make much sense to someone from, say, the Sudan.

The Special Educational Needs and Disability Act 2001 (SENDA), extended the coverage of the Disability Discrimination Act (DDA) (1995) to education, and the teaching and learning components came into force in September 2002. The DDA 1995 (Amendment) Regulations were issued in 2003 and the legislation will be further amended in Oct 2004 with the introduction of the further DDA (Amendment) Regulations, when all organisations providing goods, facilities or services to the public must make reasonable adjustments to overcome physical barriers which deny access to disabled people. The Act thus has significant implications for education. But the DDA is about much more than physical access. It is now more important than ever that all materials provided for all students meet high accessibility standards. Numerous guidelines exist as to what constitutes 'accessible' and we will be looking in more detail at accessibility of IT resources in Section 6.2, but all paper and audio-visual materials need to be prepared appropriately too.

Particular care needs to be taken with the type and size of font used, as well as with the layout of printed materials. In order to meet the needs of a wide range of students, it is advisable to provide an electronic version of all documents at the same time as hard copies. Students can then adjust the content to an appropriate font for themselves.

Such advice is relevant to a whole range of documents produced for students (and staff). At the time of writing, the University of Leeds is preparing an 'Accessible Information Policy', which will address such issues.

Task 5

Evaluation of printed and audio-visual materials
**This would be a good point at which to re-examine the course materials used in one of the modules on which you teach. First consider whether there is a good balance in any materials that contain examples of human activities or achievements with regard to gender, culture, sexuality, and disability. Secondly, use two of the three University of Leeds SDDU Accessible Learning and Teaching guides to check if the materials meet accessibility standards: 'Preparation of Printed Learning Materials' and 'Preparation of Audio-visual learning Materials (1)'
(see: www.ldu.leeds.ac.uk/lt/equality.htm).**

Commentary

Clearly it would be just as inappropriate in most materials to see only 'black' faces, or have every character in all case-studies being gay or disabled. However, looked at overall, there needs to be reference to a cross-section of people that reflects the reality in the population.

Materials prepared following the Leeds guides will benefit ALL students, not just disabled students. In general, good practice for some, is good practice for all. Remember though, that there may be individual students with an assessment of study strategies and skills, for whom a very specific format of materials will be required, for example Braille. Your university disability services unit will be able to advise you on preparing these.

In addition, you need to consider the language used in your materials.

4.3 Language of learning

4.3.1 The spoken word

The amount of talking In spite of the widely held stereotype that women talk more than men, research into discourse in formal or public settings (including the classroom) has found that men frequently (but not necessarily) talk more of the time in a mixed-sex group than do women, and that men will interrupt women more often than women will interrupt men. (For a comprehensive review of research in this field see Tannen 1993). Some hold the explanation of this to be 'simply that men talk more as a way of exploiting their greater power and exercising dominance and control over women, and that they attempt to prevent women from speaking because they devalue women'. Others suggest that such a view does not take into account the idea that women and men are socialised to have different goals of interaction and therefore use talk in different ways to achieve these goals (James and Drakich 1993, p. 301). Conefrey 1997 cites the research of Goodwin 1990 and Maltz and Borker 1982. Their research suggests different ways in which boys and girls use language: boys to assert themselves, be dominant and attract an audience; and girls 'to create and maintain interpersonal relationships, criticize others in less direct ways, exert leadership less directly, and respond to the speech of others' (Conefrey, p. 329).

Whatever the reasons for the difference we need to be aware of the potential consequences of this in our teaching/learning groups and take steps to prevent any individual(s) dominating group discussions or question times during more formal teaching presentations.

The vocabulary of talking It is no longer acceptable to most people in our society to use language which is offensive, patronising or excluding to anyone. It is particularly important within an educational institution to set and maintain standards which are exemplary. Our students are the teachers, managers and employers of tomorrow and it is crucial that they are adequately prepared to be able to set a good example when they are in positions of influence.

That preparation comes best from our own example now, both in our day to day communication with students and in the teaching and learning which takes place both on and off campus. In addition we must be prepared to challenge the use of language by others which is inappropriate. Humour is sometimes used by lecturers and others in an attempt to provide a shared experience which emphasises inclusivity, but which can do the opposite if the humour is at the expense of 'them' (that is those in the 'out-groups' - gay people, women, Irish people, and so on) members of which may be present. Behaviour such as telling sexist, racist or homophobic jokes may not be intended to cause harm but can, in fact, be deeply offensive and should be challenged.

Care is needed in the vocabulary we choose to use in relation to several groups of people. As this is a developing area there are some words which are still acceptable to some people but not to others. There are others which are no longer acceptable at all, especially to the people to whom they refer.

Age

The terms 'old folk' and 'the elderly' are no longer regarded as acceptable; terms such as 'pensioners' and 'senior citizens' are acceptable to some but not others; but 'older people' seems to be acceptable to all. Members of Black and minority ethnic communities also use the term 'elders'.

Racial and cultural diversity

Overtly racist remarks have become unacceptable to most people over the last several years, but there are still ways in which language can be implicitly racist, often unintentionally. We can present knowledge which is culturally biased. Very often the Eurocentric viewpoint or even white Anglocentric perspective is presented as if it were universal. When members of different racial groups are referred to, people often use the term 'ethnic', as if people in minority ethnic groups were the only ones to have 'ethnicity'.

Since each of us is a member of an ethnic group (whether large or small) it is meaningless to use the term 'ethnic' on its own to describe a member of a minority rather than of a majority ethnic group. In some instances people refer to the country of origin of a person when referring to someone's ethnicity, but this is meaningless if in fact they are British. The term 'black' is the 'political' term used to describe people of Black and minority ethnic (BME) origins. It is used to describe people of African, Afro-Caribbean, or African-American origin, and people of South Asian origin as well. However, some South Asians prefer the term 'black and Asian'. (For a fuller discussion of terminology – race, ethnicity and culture – see Section 2 of the Anti-racist toolkit by Turney et al. 2002.) Many people prefer to be identified by their religious faith rather than by their racial identity – see Section 5.6.

Naming systems

When asking for someone's name it is more appropriate to ask for their first name rather than their Christian name. That said, many Chinese names have the family name first followed by the 'personal' name. In this case, it is perhaps more helpful to ask for the full name and to ask the student by which name they would prefer to be called. Many overseas students do not expect to use the first names of their teachers, since in some cultures (as in one generation back in the British culture) this would be viewed as disrespectful. (For more information see the HM Land Registry guide 'Cultural Diversity'.)

Using other languages

You could sometimes use languages other than English to greet your student groups, when you know that there are students present for whom their first language is not English, or in emailing individual students. For a list of forms of greetings in many languages see the following websites:
www.elite.net/%7Erunner/jennifers/hello.htm
and **www.travlang.com/languages/search.html**

Disability

The writers of the Open University's Equal Opportunities Guide to Language and Image 1993 suggest that ' ... by using language with care you can embrace your varied audience rather than unthinkingly alienate parts of it' (p. 11) and that it is easy to use language from an able-bodied point of view when talking about disabled people in general.

They suggest that it is better to use the term 'disabled people' rather than 'people with disabilities' since the former 'emphasises that people are disabled by a society that doesn't accommodate them, not by their condition itself'. They stress as well, however, the need to avoid being patronising about disabled people and to avoid using stereotypes.

Sexuality

The term 'lesbians and gay men' is preferred to 'homosexual', and an increasing number of people now identify themselves as 'bisexual'. It is more appropriate to use the term 'partner' rather than 'spouse' since the former includes members of all 'couples', not just married people.

Gender

It is perhaps in the area of gender where there is continuing resistance to using inclusive language. Many persist in the use of the male noun and pronoun only, on the grounds that this also encompasses the female. Whilst this is regarded by some as technically true, the term 'man' still conjures up the picture of the adult male person, and the term 'he' often makes it unclear who is meant. According to Miller and Swift 1995 the word 'man' meant person or human being in Old English and when used of an individual was equally applicable to either sex. It was parallel to the Latin 'homo' – a member of the human species. However, since the eighteenth century the modern, narrow sense of 'man' has been firmly established as the predominant one (p. 12). Many believe that the exclusive use of 'he' may lead to the perpetuation of the subjugation of women.

As Miller and Swift point out ' ... reality affects language and is, in turn, affected by it' (p. 3) and that research on the use of 'man' and 'men' indicates that the words tend to call up images of male people only, not female people or females and males together (p. 13). The use of 'person' or 'people' is now common. Alternatives to the male pronoun, such as 'he or she', or 'she or he', or 's/he' (in the written form) are in frequent use, and 'they' or 'their' is an acceptable shorter term meaning 'he or she' or 'his or her'.

Often terms used for women are patronising. A good judge as to what might be acceptable is to consider the equivalent words used of men. For instance, women are patronised when the terms 'girl' or 'lady' are used in circumstances where 'boy' and 'gentleman' would not be used. Too often the male word is taken to be the norm and the female is regarded as a deviation from the norm, and is often the diminutive of it, for example actor/actress, hero/heroine, usher/usherette. There is no reason why the first word cannot be used as inclusive and as gender neutral. There are many examples where this is already the case, for example doctor, nurse, traffic warden, bus driver, and so on. Other gender neutral words have come into more common usage in recent years, for example: spokesperson, headteacher, police officer, sales assistant, firefighter, and so on.

Consider:
How will you manage unacceptable comments and attitudes from students during teaching and learning activities?

4.3.2 The written word
It is obviously just as important to ensure that the vocabulary used in written materials is also appropriate. This will apply to any materials produced as supplementary to lectures and seminars for courses that are taught face to face, as well as to materials produced for open and distance learning. It is also important to keep all written texts (including information leaflets and application forms) as straight-forward as possible. Although academic texts have traditionally been written in a rather formal style using the third person (to imply objectivity perhaps?) it is better to write learning materials in a friendlier style, as if you were addressing the students in person, for example by using 'I' or 'we' and 'you'. This helps improve the relationship between the writer and their readers, thus making the latter feel more included.

The level of difficulty of the materials will obviously depend upon the level of the course for which they are being written, but even higher level course material can be written in a simple, easy to follow way. In the 1986 edition of Sir Ernest Gowers' 'The complete plain words' (originally published in 1954) the editors Sidney Greenbaum and Janet Whitcut add (p. 198) 'We frequently suggest replacements that follow the rules "Be short, be simple, be human"'. Although specialist vocabulary is necessary in most subject disciplines it is good to offer explanations of the meaning of words and acronyms the first time they are used, or to include a glossary and/or list of abbreviations. In these ways people are not excluded because they do not have the benefit of prior knowledge. In other words, you need to avoid denying students 'epistemological access'.

[vi] The term 'Black and minority ethnic (BME)' is used to denote members of minority ethnic groups. Whilst not a satisfactory term to use in many ways it is a commonly accepted 'short-hand' term used in the UK to denote those from Asian, Afro-Caribbean and many other origins.

Section 5:

Delivery of the curriculum

If all students are to be able to achieve their potential they need to be able to participate fully in the curriculum.

5.1 Teaching methods

'Variety', it is said, 'is the very spice of life' (William Cowper's 'The Task Poem' written in 1785). Perhaps this could be said to be as true of teaching and learning as of any other field. By using different teaching methods within each module you will hopefully appeal at some stage to everyone's favourite. Consideration of Neil Fleming's VARK test for visual, auditory and/or kinesthetic preferences would suggest that including methods that use a variety of media is a good thing. The test includes a questionnaire which can be used to discover, not the particular strengths of individuals, but their preferences for the ways in which they like to receive and give information. Honey and Mumford's Learning Styles work suggests that different students learn better when they can best exploit their preferred styles of learning. For example, some students need regular periods of time built in for reflection on what they have learned, or to theorise about the possible outcomes of different actions, whilst others prefer to jump straight into an activity. (See Appendix 1 for details of these tools to discover learning preferences and styles of your students).

The overall message is one of flexibility of delivery in diversity. [For specific practical suggestions of teaching and learning activities you might like to see Lewis and Habeshaw 1990 and for examples of good practice on a subject by subject basis see Ryan 1997, pp. 35–67.]

5.1.1 Large and small group teaching

With increasing student numbers there is a growing tendency to use the mass lecture as the main or sole method of teaching on some programmes of study.

This is not necessarily the most appropriate method for many students, especially those who might have difficulties with note-taking for a variety of reasons. Seminar/tutorial time, where traditionally the student could ask for clarification of any points which were not clear in the lecture, is being eroded, and the opportunity for thorough exploration of tangential points of intellectual interest are a luxury rarely available. Independent learning, making more extensive use of course materials, whilst compensating in part for this loss, cannot replace the stimulus which can be present in a small group discussion.

One of the female overseas students featured on the UKCOSA 1994 video expresses regret at the lack of opportunity for small group discussion in which she could have learned more of other students' ideas. James and Dovaston 1991 (cited in Ashcroft et al. 1996, p. 25) found that, as well as learner-centred learning, small group activity and the acknowledgement of prior experience were generally helpful factors for adult learners. Research suggests that male students would be less likely to feel the loss of such 'connected' learning, whilst female students would more likely mourn the passing of frequent opportunities for group work. That said, since some students/tutors are inclined to dominate group discussions, such a method of learning is not necessarily always a positive experience either, so care needs to be taken with the design and management of small group work.

5.1.2 Overseas students

Kinnell 1990 found that generally overseas students were new to discussion-based learning, but that, although it required greater competency in what for them was a foreign language, it was welcomed by most as a positive development in their learning experience (pp. 53–4).

Many of the overseas students interviewed for another research project, however, said that 'they feel they don't exist for home students and have difficulty joining in group work' (Ryan 1997, p. 25). Lecturers in this project did find that 'sensitive intervention ... can help international students participate more fully in groups and in the classroom' (p. 26). One of the overseas students featured on the UKCOSA video pointed out that the English students react faster than him in tutorials because of his language difficulties, and another suggested that the English speaking students and the lecturers need to demonstrate a little patience with the students for whom English is not their first language.

A study conducted in an Australian university (Wright and Lander 2003) examined the differences in verbal interaction between students in mono-ethnic and bi-ethnic groups, made up of two students from each ethnic cohort – Australian-born Anglo-European and overseas-born South East Asian students – during mandatory class-based projects. The key finding suggests that the South East Asian students were inhibited in terms of their verbal participations when with Australian students. Although it could be concluded from this that students should be allowed to work with those with whom they feel most comfortable, since they learn content more effectively, the authors acknowledge that another type of learning 'how to function effectively in intercultural encounters' is also important.

Their rather depressing conclusion is that:

'Universities are deluding themselves if they believe that the presence of international students on campus contributes to the internationalisation of higher education. The findings reported here demonstrate that there can be little reassurance that arranging groups of mixed-ethnic origin membership will lead to profitable interaction.'
(Wright and Lander 2003, p. 252)

They suggest that students need to be taught the skills to work effectively in mixed ethnic groups, if intercultural interaction is to benefit student learning, and acknowledge that much more research is needed in this area.

Consider:
How will you encourage/manage ethnic mix in small group tutorials? How will you manage resistance when it does occur? How will you teach the skills to challenge discriminatory practice?

As in the above case of mixed-race groups, special efforts need to be made to accommodate the requirements of all of your students. Some of their needs can be met more easily than others.

5.2 Meeting students' practical needs
There are many aspects of students' practical needs which could be taken into account when planning courses. For example, mature students can experience difficulties attending early morning classes or classes after 3.00 p.m. because of family commitments. Such difficulties are exacerbated when school holidays or staff training days do not coincide with university holidays. Although the distance learning mode might be considered more flexible for mature students, research has indicated that students (especially women students) still value the few group sessions or one-to-one tutorials which might be available to them. Finding crèche accommodation for pre-school children on an occasional basis might actually prove more problematic for students than getting a regular place for a child and attending classes as a full-time student on a course taught face to face on campus.

Part-time students (and some full-time ones) may well be coping with the demands of a job as well. There is little that a teacher can do here, except to adopt a sympathetic attitude and make due allowances. Students of particular religious groups often request that classes or exams are not scheduled on particular days or at particular times, for example Muslim and Jewish Holidays, Friday afternoons when Muslim prayers are held, Fridays after sunset when the Jewish Shabbat begins, and so on (for more details see Weller, 1992.) The physical needs of some disabled students must, of course, also be taken into account.

Task 6

To what extent do you think that you should make allowances for the practical needs of particular groups of students? For example, is it right to allow late submission of essays of a mature student because of domestic problems, for example a sick child, or to avoid scheduling an exam on a Saturday out of consideration for Jewish students? You might like to make a note of a few of your thoughts on this issue, possibly for discussion with others at a later date.

Commentary

This is a potential source of conflict for tutors, particularly for those responsible for the timetable. Incidents such as whether or not to make allowances for family problems must surely be judged by the individual tutor on individual merit, but there are no easy answers to this one. Even where an individual teacher would like to effect change in this area they may not be able to because of other internal or external factors. There are, however, some areas where you are now required by law to meet the needs of your students. It is perhaps when considering the needs of disabled students that the greatest thought needs to be given to teaching methods and to the media used. It is also the area where most resources are available to help staff address the issues (see below and the Resources Section at the end of this guide).

5.3 Disabled students

Disability is one of the most significant areas in which there has been a shift from issues of access alone to an inclusive curriculum. Writing in 1999, Parker stated:

'Now more disabled students are in the sector, it is clear that they experience many difficulties in accessing the curriculum in all its aspects. It is also becoming apparent that there is a need to ensure that innovations in learning and teaching enable the learning of *all* students and do not create new barriers for those with disabilities.' (emphasis added) (Parker 1999, p. 19).

Recent legislation has lead to an increase in the speed of change in practice in the area of inclusivity and disability.

However as Adams (2000 cited in GDN 2001d, p. 12) states: '... we must avoid falling into the trap of viewing disabled students as a homogeneous group. The process of designing an "accessible curriculum" for one disabled student will undoubtedly be different, and in some cases at total odds, with that of other individuals.' The Special Educational Needs and Disability Act (SENDA) 2001 came into force in September 2002. The Act uses a wide definition of disabled person, including people with a wide range of impairments. Under the legislation it is illegal to:

- refuse to serve, or
- offer a lower standard of service, or
- offer the service on worse terms to a disabled student.

'Discrimination against disabled applicants or students can take place in either of two ways:

- by treating them "less favourably" than other people, or
- by failing to make a "reasonable adjustment" when they are placed at a "substantial disadvantage" compared to other people for a reason relating to their disability.' (Disability Rights Commission 2003c, p. 4)

This means that if a disabled student finds it unreasonably difficult to use a service, an educational institution has to make reasonable changes to that service. It applies to all aspects of services provided by HEIs, including those related to teaching and learning, from the more traditional methods of delivering lectures to e-learning. 'The legislation aims to ensure that disabled people have equal opportunities to benefit from, and contribute to the learning and services available in higher education institutions. The legislation protects disabled students in all aspects of their studies' (DRC 2003e, p. 1). It covers all students, whether 'full and part-time; postgraduate and undergraduate; home, EU and international; students on short courses and taster courses; students taking evening classes and day schools; distance and e-learning students; and students undertaking only part of a course or visiting from another institution' (DRC 2003e, p. 3).

Accessibility to on-campus facilities for students with mobility difficulties has perhaps been the most high-profile, visible adjustment that HEIs have made, but accessibility of other forms are creating a major challenge to all institutions too. The accessibility of e-learning resources and to other web-based information and services has placed a heavy resource demand on institutions, but the resulting changes in practice are beneficial not only to visually impaired students but have improved the usability of web resources for all. Consideration must also be paid to the needs of disabled students in lab work, practicals, field trips and work placements. Adjustments may also be needed when it comes to examinations and other forms of assessment. (Many of these issues are addressed in more detail later in this book in Sections 5.8 & 5.9 and Sections 6 and 7.)

Disabled people have the same range of academic ability as others of their age and have the right to benefit from the same educational opportunities. It is very often not a person's impairment which prevents them participating fully in education but the lack of the appropriate equipment or environment (Corlett and Cooper 1992). For a disabled student entering an HEI an 'Assessment of need' is conducted with them prior to the start of their course, and any requirements for support are identified. A written statement is then produced which is available to all academic staff. (A similar process is undertaken if a student becomes disabled in the course of their studies.) Whilst the specific needs of each disabled student must be identified on an individual basis, it may be helpful to briefly outline at this point some information about disabled students.

Visually impaired students
The vast majority of visually impaired students will have some useful sight – only a very small proportion (about 4 per cent) are totally blind and unable to see at all. A small percentage of people with a visual impairment will also be deaf or hard of hearing.

Deaf and hearing impaired students
Most d/Deaf or hearing impaired people have some ability to hear. Some may have been born d/Deaf – others may have become d/Deaf gradually or suddenly as a child or adult.

Pre-lingually d/Deaf people (that is those who became d/Deaf before learning to speak and read) find it much harder than others to learn spoken and written language.

As is explained by the authors of GDN 2001c, a distinction is made between deaf and Deaf people.

'**Deaf** with capital D is used ... to define people with severe to profound d/Deafness, who regard themselves as belonging to a cultural and linguistic minority.'

'**deaf** with lower-case d refers to people with severe to profound deafness, who choose to speak and lip-read (also known as "Oral deaf ").' (GDN 2001c)

Those in the first category communicate in British Sign Language (BSL), using interpreters to facilitate communication with hearing people. 'BSL is the first or preferred language of more than 70,000 Deaf people in the United Kingdom. Like sign languages used in other parts of the world, it is a full and complete language in its own right, with its own grammar, vocabulary and syntax, and is totally separate from English' (p. 5).

There is, however, a profound shortage of trained BSL teachers – only 175 listed in 2003 by the Council for the Advancement of Communication with Deaf People (CACDP). Frustrated by this shortage in its attempts to appoint staff to meet the needs of d/Deaf students on University of Leeds courses and fulfil the requirements of SENDA, staff at the Equality Unit at the university have worked with the School of Modern Languages and Cultures to design a new masters level course, which started in October 2003, MA Interpreting British Sign Language (MAIBSL), a first in the UK. This will hopefully mean that there will soon be more qualified people available to offer support to Deaf students.

Students with medical conditions
Some students will have long term or permanent medical conditions that may affect their learning capabilities.

Some examples are: epilepsy, diabetes, ME, hayfever, haemophilia, sickle cell anaemia, cystic fibrosis, HIV, AIDS, asthma, heart and other chronic conditions. (Skill 1997 p. 99) You may well be advised to know who to contact should an emergency arise. The student is probably the best person to ask about simple procedures to follow should certain symptoms manifest themselves, although many students will prime a fellow student in the same group on how to help if necessary. Such an example might be if someone who has epilepsy has a seizure.

Students with physical impairment

Students may be disabled if they have one of a number of conditions, for example: muscular dystrophy, brittle bones, arthritis, polio, multiple sclerosis, spina bifida, cerebral palsy or hydrocephalus. Some students with physical impairment may also have mobility impairment. The basic ability to learn is unaffected in most people with a physical impairment, although people who have sustained a head injury of some description may or may not also have specific learning difficulties, including perceptual, cognitive or memory problems of various kinds. (Skill 1997 p. 103)

Students with language and speech difficulties

Some students may have difficulties communicating through speech. This may result from illnesses such as strokes or may be associated with other disabilities such as cerebral palsy. In some cases the causes may not be known. Some students may only have a problem when talking about abstract rather than concrete matters, other students may have a severe stutter at all times.

Students with specific learning difficulties (including dyslexia)

The most frequent specific learning difficulty is with reading and writing, sometimes called dyslexia. Some people may have difficulty with numbers. The cause of the difficulty may not be known. It is likely to make learning more difficult, but does not affect overall academic ability as it doesn't reflect a lack of intelligence, though it may be interpreted as such by some people.

Some students who have had difficulties learning in the past, perhaps before dyslexia was diagnosed, may lack confidence. Some people with specific learning difficulties may have problems in areas other than reading and writing, for example perceptual problems, sequencing, and hand-eye control. (Skill 1997 p. 111)

Consider:

You believe that a student may be dyslexic (because of oral contributions in class or because of the standard of their written work) but the student has not informed anyone that they are experiencing problems. What action (if any) would you take?

Students with mental ill-health

The DDA 1995 Act also includes mental health. ' "Disability" is defined as a physical or mental impairment that has a substantial and long-term adverse effect on a person's ability to carry out normal, day-to-day activities. If a mental illness is clinically well recognised, it will count as a mental impairment under the Act' (mindOUT 2003).

The level of mental health problems among students is increasing rapidly according to the Heads of the University Counselling Services (HUCS 1999) and the Royal College of Psychiatrists (RCPsych 2003). Some people experience mental ill-health temporarily, perhaps as the result of too much stress or a bereavement. Other conditions are longer term but the person may experience periods of good health interspersed with poor health. Assumptions cannot be made about any student who has declared mental ill-health, as a situation which might affect one student may not affect another in the same way. Students may need help from the medical centre or from the Student Counselling Service. Students may suffer side effects from medication which may affect their learning, including participation in class discussion. They may also need reasonable adjustment in the learning and teaching situation, and may qualify for the disabled students' allowance (DSA).

Our response
None of the above impairments need to produce barriers to learning which are insurmountable. Detailed help and advice will be available for staff in most HEIs, for example from a disability services unit. A handbook will also often be available from such an office and might include, among other things, ideas for improving the learning experiences of students with specific disabilities. In addition, various nationally produced materials are also available. (In addition to Corlett and Cooper 1992 and Skill 1997 see the details of SWANDS and UWIC below. See also Section 6 for information about meeting the IT needs of disabled students.)

Some of these resources may be held in the disability services unit. Information and help is also available from a number of specialist organisations. (For details of such organisations see Skill 1997 Part Three, and the Resources Section at the end of this guide). Resources are available at the University of Leeds (2004a and b) for helping staff and students.) Many HEIs will have an on-going programme of staff development events concerned with all aspects of student welfare, including the needs of disabled students. Staff should also feel confident about asking students themselves about what their requirements are.

The SWANDS guide: 'SENDA Compliance in Higher Education' (2002) provides a comprehensive guidance resource and audit tool for examining current practice in the broad areas of admissions, accessible learning, teaching and assessment for disabled students. 'It focuses upon the responsibilities of the individual and the institution to meet the requirements of the post-16 sections of SENDA' (p. 7). The authors emphasise the need for 'parity of experience [for disabled students] through embedded, consistent practice rather than "bolt on" or ad hoc provision' (pp. 8–9) and for 'an orientation towards mainstreaming inclusive practice' (p. 9) created by anticipatory action, rather than in response to individual students.

The SWANDS guide is liberally and helpfully scattered with 'What students say about current practice' and 'What staff say about current practice'.

It also provides examples and checklists of good practice and additional sources of information as it works through the issues from 'Course development, programme planning, approval and review'; through document preparation (printing, visual and electronic); 'Lectures, seminars and tutorials'; 'Fieldwork'; 'Laboratories, workshops and other practice-based environments'; 'Placement learning'; and 'Assessment'. It includes in the appropriate places, the relevant precepts from the QAA 1999 'Code of Practice for Students with Disabilities' and the DRC 2002b 'DDA Code of Practice'. I recommend that you download a free copy of it from the University of Plymouth website (see References for details).

A complementary guide is the one produced by the UWIC (University of Wales Institute, Cardiff) 'Accessible curricula: good practice for all' by Doyle and Robson 2002. This is also freely available in pdf format (see References). As the authors say ' … meeting the needs of students with disabilities and/or learning difficulties has shifted away from being an optional add-on extra to becoming a part of core activities of higher education providers' (p. i). As stated in the preface:

'Using this Book will assist you in producing "barrier-free" course materials and to deliver them appropriately. This term "barrier-free" is taken from the "universal design" literature, the underlying principle being that the full range of users should be considered at the design stage. In doing so, there will be "built-in" access for a wide range of users with or without disabilities.' (Doyle and Robson 2002, p. iii)

Many teaching and learning strategies and approaches that are adopted to meet the needs of disabled students are simple extensions of good practice and will benefit all students. For example, dyslexic students or students with a visual impairment may prefer to receive a prioritised reading list before the start of their course so that they can concentrate on reading the essential texts. This could benefit all students. Another example is that lectures may be recorded on audio or video tape so that students who may not easily follow every word at normal speed or who cannot make notes because of physical difficulties may listen to the lecture again later.

This too could be of wider benefit, not only to disabled students, and especially to those who learn in a more reflective mode. Many minor modifications to teaching intended to assist disabled students can help all students' learning, for example: clearer diction, the use of handouts to summarise the main points in a class, better lighting or soundproofing, and so on. Flexible delivery is a prerequisite for responding to individual learning needs.

Task 7

Check out your practice against the third University of Leeds SDDU Accessible Learning and Teaching guides 'Delivering Teaching and Supporting Learning' (see: www.ldu.leeds.ac.uk/lt/equality.htm).

Task 8

Check out the current programme of staff development events at your institution concerned with student welfare and consider attending a session which is relevant to the particular needs of any students whom you have in your groups. Do you, in fact, know the needs of your students?

5.4 Mature students

Particular consideration needs to be given to the learning abilities of mature students. Whilst it is not desirable to perpetuate the myth of 'You can't teach an old dog new tricks' (indeed it needs to be dispelled!) it is appropriate to consider how best to facilitate the most effective learning for older students. Whilst physiological decline does affect learning, by reducing the effectiveness of sensory stimulation, the effects are not usually significant until after the age of 60. Although eyesight declines because of structural changes in the lens, usually around the age of 40, it is not until there are also changes in the retina, around 60, that the decline becomes educationally significant. Similarly, hearing often begins to fade during the thirties and gradually deteriorates thereafter. This loss, particularly in terms of speech perception, can become serious some time between the late forties and late seventies and is affected by the level of background noise and other interruptions. Attention to the arrangement of seating, to lighting and to the

use of audio-visual aids can help alleviate such physiological problems.

A more significant decline is associated with memory. (See Child 1993 Chapter 6: learning and memory.) When considering the effects of age on memory it is useful to divide it into short-term and long-term. Although the capacity of short-term memory (normally seven items) does not appear to vary over time, a decline does become noticeable when the student is required to manipulate the data held in short-term memory, and in particular when they are also attempting to deal with fresh incoming data. You could, therefore, try to reduce the amount of memorising required of a mature student. This could be done, for example, by displaying written instructions rather than expecting the student to deal with an activity whilst also trying to remember verbal instructions. Assessment could also be biased away from 'memory test' techniques, for example by the introduction of more 'open book' examinations or various forms of coursework.

Long-term memory appears to have an almost infinite capacity. Accommodation of ever greater quantities of learnt skills and knowledge over a lifetime is, therefore, not a problem. Where mature students do appear to be at a disadvantage is in the acquisition of new material for long-term storage. This may well be linked to the growing problems of processing new information through short-term memory into long-term memory. You can reduce this disadvantage by presenting new stimuli so that they are readily assimilated into the mature student's existing schemata. This may well be easier than it sounds, since these schemata are likely to be more extensive than for younger students. Indeed having mature students in your groups can be a very positive thing. You can make use of their experience and accumulated insights in planning lessons, and by encouraging their contributions.

Learning ability of all students is clearly affected by intelligence. Whilst this is a widely used concept and one which is difficult to define, one approach which is helpful in a consideration of ageing is Cattell's division of intelligence into fluid and crystallised, and

Horn's research into the growth and decline of both (see Cattell 1963 and Horn 1967). Fluid intelligence is relatively independent of education and other experience and is concerned with conceptual ability and reasoning. It is essentially innate, being based on the given neurophysiological structure. Crystallised intelligence, on the other hand, results from the interplay of fluid intelligence with our environment. It increases with education and life experience and is applicable to information processing, comprehension and social skills.

Both fluid and crystallised intelligence improve during childhood, adolescence and into the twenties. The evidence suggests that fluid intelligence then begins to slowly decline as a result of physiological decay and this decay will slowly continue through life. Crystallised intelligence, however, continues to increase until very late in life. The rate and extent of increase is largely determined by the extent to which the individual exercises her or his mind through their lifetime. The mature student then operates a trade-off between a declining fluid intelligence and a stable, or growing, crystallised intelligence. Accumulated wisdom takes the place of innate brilliance.

The implications of this research for the teacher of mature students is that the decline in fluid intelligence may cause problems when dealing with new concepts. However, since our success in solving problems depends on the prior acquisition of knowledge and experience, the mature student will be better equipped to learn in a problem solving 'case study' learning environment than younger students. We can, therefore, offer learning methods which will suit our students.

Overall, then, we have a picture of the mature student who, although needing our help to overcome some problems created by physiological decline, is nevertheless still very able to learn and who, because of their very maturity, is in a position to make a very positive contribution to any class of students.

5.5 Race

The size of the minority ethnic population was 4.6 million in 2001 or 7.9 per cent of the total population of the United Kingdom (2001 Census). Indians (1.8 per cent) were the largest minority group, followed by Pakistanis (1.3 per cent), those of Mixed ethnic backgrounds (1.2 per cent), Black Caribbeans (1.0 per cent), Black Africans (0.8 per cent) and Bangladeshis (0.5 per cent). The remaining minority ethnic groups each accounted for less than 0.5 per cent but together accounted for a further 1.4 per cent of the UK population. 14.5 per cent of students in UK HEIs in 2002–03 were UK domiciled minority ethnic students. Many HEIs also have a significant proportion of overseas students (for example 12 per cent of Leeds students in 2003–04). Under the terms of the Race Relations (Amendment) Act 2000, every HEI had to prepare (by 31 May 2002) a race equality policy, setting out the steps required to tackle discrimination and promote race equality and good race relations. They also have to assess the impact of policies on ethnic minority students and staff; monitor recruitment and progress of ethnic minority students and staff; and set out in the race equality policy the arrangements for publishing the policy and results of assessment and monitoring. There are many guides to help HEIs improve practice in this area.

In 2002 the Commission for Racial Equality (CRE) (established following the Race Relations Act 1976) produced a statutory code of practice (CRE 2002a), and four non-statutory guides, to help authorities in England and Wales meet their duty. One of the non-statutory guides is for institutions of further and higher education (CRE 2002b). Included in the list of benefits of meeting the general duty to promote race equality is to: 'Create a positive atmosphere, where there is a shared commitment to value diversity and respect difference' (p. 4).

'The Institutional Racism in Higher Education Toolkit Project', was a HEFCE funded Innovations Project led by staff in the Centre for Ethnicity and Racism Studies, Department of Sociology and Social Policy at the University of Leeds, and which used Leeds as a case study.

The toolkit 'aims to assist institutions in the process of anti-racist and race equality planning and action by providing conceptual and methodological "tools" ' (quoted from their website). It is available as an online resource (for details see: Turney et al. 2002).

Section 4 of the Toolkit – 'Anti-racist strategies' – includes sub-sections on 'Teaching and learning' (4.6) and 'Research' (4.7), as well as on 'Employment' (4.4) and 'Student recruitment, support and transition to employment' (4.5) and provides a lot of useful information relevant to curriculum issues. It addresses many of the questions raised in the CRE guide (2002b) and quoted above. Section 4.5 provides 'ideas and strategies for incorporating and promoting anti-racist and race equality measures into student admissions, ... counselling and careers services' and encourages HEIs to address issues of 'inequalities faced by Black and minority ethnic students and graduates in the employment market' (p. 87). In the Summary of Section 4.6 the authors urge 'institutions to reflect upon assessment procedures and the curriculum in order to take into consideration the various ways in which current content and practice may discriminate against Black and minority ethnic students via the use of inappropriate resources and a eurocentric perspective' (p. 91). They ask the following question: 'Are the literatures, music, arts, histories and religions, etc, of 'non-Western'/'not-white' peoples periphalised and tokenised in the curriculum ... [or] ... positioned as inferior, primitive?'.

Task 9

To consider your own practice in this area, use the checklist of 'Key questions to consider' that is provided in Section 4.6a of the Anti-racist Toolkit and take a look at the 'Sample Targets and Positive Action Strategies for Teaching and Learning' in Section 4.6d (www.leeds.ac.uk/cers/toolkit/toolkit.htm)

A tutor on a media studies course tries to promote ideas of anti-oppression within her module by discussing current news issues as they arise, looking at the media at home and abroad (including on websites), and using them to look at wider issues. This helps to develop skills in the students to critique the media, including de-coding and criticising interpretations of race, ethnicity, gender and so on. Recent issues have included September 11th, the War in Iraq, and the Hutton Inquiry. Deconstruction of the Ian Wright/Nescafe billboard ad has also been used to open up issues of race, class, globalisation, the use of images and so on.

The Race Relations Act 1976 made discrimination unlawful on the grounds of race, colour, nationality, ethnic or national origin in respect of provision of employment and the provision of goods and services. Although the RRAA 2000 strengthened the 1976 Act, it did not extend it to include discrimination on the grounds of religion or belief, creating the situation where Jews, Sikhs and Gypsies were covered by the legislation, but Muslims, Hindus and Rastafarians were not. Such anomalies (with regard to employment at least) have now been addressed in recent further UK legislation, made necessary in order to comply with a new European directive, that is, the Employment Equality (Religion or Belief) Regulations 2003.

5.6 Religion or belief
A question on religion was introduced by the Office for National Statistics on the Census in England, Wales and Scotland for the first time in 2001, although such a question had been asked in Northern Ireland on previous Censuses. Although a voluntary question, over 92 per cent of people chose to answer it. Almost 77 per cent of the total population in the UK reported having a religion – the majority (72 per cent) stating that their religion was Christianity. However, although this number of people (about 42 million) identified with the Christian religion in the Census, fewer than 10 per cent attend church each week.

This seems to suggest that the vast majority of those of the Christian religion have only a nominal adherence to their religion, but it is important to remember that there are many people who, as Grace Davie 1994 puts it, 'believe without belonging'. However, 15.5 per cent of the population – a significant minority – reported having no religion, including atheists and agnostics – and perhaps indicates a growing secularisation of the formerly Christian majority.

The largest single minority religious group with which respondents identified is the Muslim religion (nearly 3 per cent – 1.6 million), a much larger percentage of whom are 'practising'. Hindus, Jews, Buddhists and people from 'Other religions' constitute a further 3 per cent of the population. A further 7.3 per cent declined to answer the question. (Office for National Statistics, 2003) The authors of the guide 'Religious literacy' (Yorkshire and Humber Assembly 2004), in challenging the false assumption that if there are anti-racist policies and practices in place there will be no more discrimination against people in religious groups, state:

'Anti-racism policies are crucial, but, where someone's primary identity is religious, it is insulting to relate to them by race and colour. Unfortunately it is possible to be anti-racist, whilst being prejudiced against religion, religious people and faith communities.' (Yorkshire and Humber Assembly 2004, p.22)

Similarly, NATFHE (2002) in the discussion document 'Discrimination on the grounds of religion or belief ' emphasise that 'many individuals locate their sense of identity **primarily** in their religious adherence, rather than their racial origin' (p. 4). Civil unrest associated with race and religion in the Summer of 2001 in the UK and in the autumn of the same year in the USA have placed the issues of religion and race high on the agenda of the governments of both countries. With the potential for an increase in Islamaphobia and indiscriminate responses to all members of all 'non-Christian' religious groups, it is crucial that we address the issue of religion or belief in the curriculum just as seriously as the issue of race.

Whilst it does not address the whole issue of discrimination, a greater understanding and awareness of people of different religions is a good starting point in encouraging greater tolerance between people of disparate groups. Although we can't all become experts on all of the different religious groups, we can familiarise ourselves with the basic tenets of most of the faiths of the people with whom we may come into contact, and by relatively minor changes in educational practice ensure that our students become familiar with them too. The NATFHE guide above, in addition to providing a model policy on culture, religion and belief (directed primarily at staffing issues) provides short introductions to the major religions.

The Diversity and Equal Opportunities Team at HM Land Registry has produced an excellent guide on religious and cultural observance, belief, language and naming systems: 'Cultural diversity', which, although intended to promote good relationships between people in the workforce, is a rich resource for all those involved in every aspect of the life of HEIs, including those coming into contact with students. After a general introduction, in which the importance of respect for non-believers is also flagged up, there is a clear and very brief outline (two to three pages) of each of eight religions, plus additional sections on naming systems and languages. Each outline includes information on: key beliefs; holy writings; holy places; holy days and festivals; diet; rites and practices; symbols and observances. SHAP (the Working Party on World Religions in Education) regularly produces a Calendar of Religious Festivals (see Resources) and some institutions, for example Leeds Metropolitan University, distribute to staff the print-based guide to religious festivals, taken from the online resource the Interfaith Calendar (see **www.interfaithcalendar.org/**)

Knowledge and understanding alone are not enough: it takes more than that to eliminate discrimination, victimisation and harassment, but by becoming acquainted with important events in the religious calendars of the various faiths you will hopefully be able at the very least to show that you are aware of them, and at best incorporate some aspect of the faith or the festival into the curriculum at the relevant time.

Tailoring is very often perceived as following a western dress code, so in a tailoring class in which there are students with a wide range of nationalities, in order to broaden and enrich the curriculum, the tutor uses a Questionnaire: 'How does your family celebrate a wedding?' This includes questions about gender, their nationality and that of their parents and grandparents, and their religion. It also asks: Where would the celebration take place? What would the bride and groom wear? Would there be a party afterwards? Would it be at a restaurant, in a hall or at home? What types of food would there be? Would there be drinks? Would there be dancing? The Questionnaire is followed by class discussion about how the students and their families celebrate a wedding and the students bring in photographs to share, to illustrate the forms of dress worn at weddings.

Only time will tell exactly how (if at all) the Employment Equality (Religion or Belief) Regulations 2003 will impact upon the curriculum in HEIs, but surely we do not need to wait for case law before implementing what we know to be basic good practice in this area, such as being aware of holy days, religious festivals and fasting periods when planning field trips, examinations, and so on. We also need to remember that the principle of non-discrimination applies to those with no religious belief or have beliefs that are not religious (for example humanism) or who are agnostic. Whatever the letter of the law is, the spirit of the law is well expressed in the following quote from the NATFHE guide (2002).

'The fact that we … live in a multi-cultural society means that we all have to compromise about how freely we express our prejudices, viewpoints and feelings about the lifestyle of others. Reasoned debate about the existence or non-existence of God obviously comes within the ambit of free speech. Academic freedom must mean freedom to explore, for example, the nature of the universe, the origins of the species, the reasons for belief and non-belief in an external First Cause. However, simple scorn and verbal abuse of someone for being *"stupid enough to believe such fairytales"* verges on impinging on the rights of others.'

'Expressing outright contempt for someone because they either do or do not drink alcohol is an attempt to impose your own cultural norms on those around you. An individual has an absolute right to choose not to have an abortion because of her religious beliefs, but no right to hurl abuse at women who exercise their right to choose abortion. There is a right to believe that God forbids sexual love between two men, but no right to distribute hate literature about gay men in the workplace.' (NATFHE 2002, pp. 14–5).

As the guide concludes: 'The challenge to form an educational environment in which "freedom of thought, conscience and religion" is a reality, but in which "the rights and freedoms" of all groups are respected is a very great one' (p. 15). Hopefully those of us working in HE today will rise to this challenge.

At the start of small group work on a transferable skills module the tutor asks each group of students to produce a poster about the things that they think will enable them to learn effectively within the group. All students then take a look at the posters of the other groups and offer each other comments using post-it notes. The tutor then facilitates a discussion, using the posters as a basis for determining a set of 'Ground Rules for Learning' for the group. In four years of running this module with very multi-cultural groups the tutor always gets consensus on the inclusion of a rule which says that they should respect each others' cultural values and beliefs in relation to learning, and another which says that it is OK to be critical of the ideas of others but not the person.

The Higher Education Academy (formerly LTSN) Subject Centres led by the Philosophical and Religious Studies Subject Centre are working on a project to explore the implications of cultural and religious issues in HE, in particular for the curriculum (for example teaching style, content, assessment and student support). They intend to provide resources that will help the HE sector to respond to their students needs in these areas.

For details of all of the Subject Centres see **www.heacademy.ac.uk/**

5.7 Sexual orientation

As with the Religion and Belief regulations, there is nothing in the Employment Equality (Sexual Orientation) Regulations 2003 that deals specifically with curriculum issues in HE, but, as the following extract from their website indicates, Stonewall, which works to achieve equality and social justice for lesbians, gays and bisexuals, believes that there are a few positive signs within education:

- All the major teaching unions are working to challenge homophobia and sexual orientation discrimination
- The Learning and Skills Council, which is now responsible for post-16 education, is issuing guidance on lesbian and gay issues [Learning and Skills Council 2003a]
- Attitudes towards lesbians and gay men among young people are becoming more and more accepting.

We still have a long way to go and while there are some examples of good practice there are also many examples of bad practice. (**www.stonewall.org.uk/stonewall/information bank/education/**)

The application of the general principles highlighted throughout this guide of providing an inclusive curriculum for all should help increase the examples of good practice in this area as in all others.

5.8 Work placements

A great deal of forethought and planning needs to go into the placing of any student into a work situation for a period of work-based learning or experience, where the learning outcomes are part of a course or period of study. This is especially true when placing disabled students. 'Providing Work Placements for Disabled Students: a Good Practice Guide for Further and Higher Education Institution' is a free booklet (DfES 2002), available as a pdf file from the DfES Lifelong Learning website or as a hard copy. It 'provides a guide to institutions' duties in regard to work placements and offers practical advice on what institutions can do to ensure quality work placement opportunities for disabled students.

It is aimed at institution staff responsible for placements: placement organisers, subject tutors and disability officers/learning support coordinators.' (Lifelong Learning website) It is suggested that in some instances the learning outcomes of the work placement may need to be adjusted for a disabled student.

As well as looking at the obvious issues of physical access to workplaces, and monitoring procedures for checking the effectiveness of work placements for disabled students, the guide recommends procedures are put in place for dealing with complaints, harassment and discrimination. It is crucial that each placement meets the individual needs of the student if it is to be successful.

A student may need additional counselling or support during what can be a very stressful period of their programme of study. Placement preparation for students and placement providers alike is necessary. The guide provides ample suggestions on this, checklists for adjustments that may be necessary, and advice on how to deal with dilemmas that may arise.

Some students from minority ethnic groups experience racism during work placements from clients, or from within the profession (Ryan 1997 p. 22). There is also the potential for women to experience sexism.

Task 10

What do you think you should do if one of your students on work placement reports an incident of racism or sexism to you?

Commentary

This is potentially a very difficult situation for an individual member of staff to handle. Unfortunately, in spite of legislation, racism and sexism are still rife in the work place and in society at large. However, it is the role of the tutor to support her/his students whilst on work placement and such incidents cannot go unchecked. Ideally any member of staff intervening in such circumstances should have specialist training. It may be more appropriate (especially for a new or relatively inexperienced tutor) to refer the case to someone else.

Try to discover if there is someone within your own department who has specialist knowledge or experience in this area: it may be the responsibility of a 'placements' officer. If not, you may feel if such a situation did arise that it would be necessary to seek help and support yourself from your university's Equal Opportunities Office. You might find it helpful to discuss this issue with your mentor (if on a recognised training course) or your Head of Department who will know of the procedures which should be followed. NB Similar help may be required to deal with racism or sexism within any of your teaching groups.

5.9 Fieldwork

A related area to work placements for disabled students is that of providing appropriate fieldwork for a disabled student to fulfil all of their course requirements (and to have the opportunity for them to benefit from the whole experience that fieldwork provides). Fieldwork has been described as: 'a structural and relevant learning experience which takes place outside the classroom' (GDN 2001d, p. 1). One of the HEFCE 'Improving Provision for Disabled Students Funding Programme' projects is the 'Learning Support for Disabled Students Undertaking Fieldwork and Related Activities' conducted by the Geography Discipline Network, a consortium of old and new universities, based at the University of Gloucester. One result of the project are six web-based guides – one general one looking at the issues of providing learning support for disabled students (GDN 2001a) and five relating to support for students with particular impairments. The guides, which provide advice for staff before, during and after fieldwork, are downloadable and printable from the website and a set of hard copies can also be purchased (see References Section of this guide under GDN for details). The series is excellent and the guides are full of pertinent advice, case studies and cameos from staff and students, which will be useful to all staff working with disabled and non-disabled students.

In the general GDN guide the authors take a detailed look at barriers to disabled students doing fieldwork and various strategies for overcoming obstacles.

They explore attitudinal, institutional and organisational system barriers, as well as physical barriers and suggest a range of approaches currently taken by institutions – from adjusting the learning outcomes of the fieldwork, through adjusting fieldtrips or destinations, to modifying practices, or offering alternatives such as surrogate or virtual trips (see for example Jenkins 2003). Such changes may need to be made for the whole group if an individual disabled student is to be fully included in the curriculum or for the individual alone.

The authors point out that on some occasions compromises may have to be made. They cite the work of Parker (1999) who advocates that 'the curriculum should be designed holistically from the outset to maximise inclusivity' (GDN 2002a, p. 22). As they suggest, discussion is key to the whole process of inclusivity:

'Facilitating access to the full curriculum needs to consider each key element of the formal and informal curriculum, so that discussion of appropriate arrangements and expectations can take place with full knowledge on both the part of the whole staff team, and the disabled student(s).' (GDN 2001a, p. 27).

This is clearly good practice re all curriculum design and delivery. As the authors acknowledge, many of the adjustments that need to be made for disabled students for fieldwork will benefit all students.
Parker (1999) p. 20 emphasises the importance of the use of appropriate learning outcomes to specify precisely what a student will be able to do on completion of a course or unit of study. This shifts the focus away from specifying 'activities, processes or tutor intentions' and onto exactly what the student needs to achieve. The close relationship between learning outcomes and assessment clearly means that an appropriate version of an assessment can be selected for an individual student to demonstrate that they have achieved the learning outcomes. Creative thinking with regards to these two elements can go a long way to creating an inclusive curriculum.

One example of changing the learning outcome to a more inclusive one is provided in the

DRC's 'Learning and Teaching Good Practice Guide':

'A programme specification required students to show "competence in handling particular chemicals". This was an unnecessary barrier to students with manual dexterity problems who used assistants to undertake practical work under instruction. The specification was changed to refer to "understanding how to handle particular chemicals".'
(Disability Rights Commission 2003c, p. 7).

Parker 1999, p. 20 draws attention to the need for adjustment to assessment tasks for assessing key skills or core competencies for students with sensory impairments, so that they can demonstrate their communication competencies in an appropriate way. This is particular pertinent to simulation and role-play exercises.

The whole of the guide 'Providing Learning Support for d/Deaf Students Undertaking Fieldwork and Related Activities' includes useful advice for staff working with d/Deaf students in all educational contexts, not just on field trips. Indeed the editors of the whole series, Phil Gravestock and Mick Healey, state:

'The advantage of focusing on fieldwork is that many of the issues faced by disabled students in higher education are magnified in this form of teaching and learning. If the barriers to full participation by everyone can be reduced or overcome it is likely that our awareness of the obstacles to their full participation in other learning activities will be heightened and the difficulties of overcoming the barriers will be lessened.' (GDN 2001c, p. ii)

Chapter four of the guide concerned with d/Deaf students provides information on 'd/Deaf Etiquette and Hints for Effective Communication' - useful in all learning and teaching situations and the authors point out that although some d/Deaf students can lip read as an aid to interpreting what is being said, it is extremely difficult and tiring to do and is an unreliable method to use on its own.
Chapter eight looks at improving learning before and after fieldwork and Chapter nine answers in the affirmative the question 'Could Good Fieldwork for Deaf Students Mean Good Fieldwork for All?'.

'Accommodating the differing needs of all students is an obligation on all teachers. Teaching and learning can be enriched for all concerned when this is done creatively and in partnership with students. d/Deaf and hearing-impaired students are one group amongst many with distinctive needs, but they are not the only such group. Any group of fieldwork students will include people with a range of abilities and disabilities and with particular needs. The best teaching of fieldwork will seek to find out and work with those needs.' (GDN 2001c, p. 18)

As reported in SWANDS 2002, p. 8, the single largest category of disability is dyslexia. There is growing consensus however that general good teaching practice can provide an inclusive curriculum that benefits all students. As stated in GDN 2001d:

'Without sacrificing academic rigour or standards, academics will need to think more imaginatively about the different ways in which different students might be enabled to demonstrate their achievement of the intended learning outcomes for the programme, module or field exercise.' (GDN 2001d, p.17).

The application of the ideas included in these guides for disabled students on fieldwork will help improve the experience for ALL students.

In summary, through imaginative and careful design of all aspects of the curriculum, it is possible to deliver a curriculum that is inclusive for all.

Section 6:

Use of information and communication technologies (ICTs)

One way in which many institutions are coping with greater student numbers is in the increasing use of ICTs both for teaching/learning purposes and for some assessment. Such approaches can also provide the element of flexibility needed in terms of place, pace and time of study by many students. Activities range from group work on the intranet, through emailed one-to-one tutorials for distance learning students, to self-assessment questions on computer (and many more). This serves the dual purpose of reducing staff contact (real) time with students and equipping students with ever increasing IT skills. This is dependent of course upon good initial training being available for those students who do not possess appropriate skills at the time of enrollment and upon the availability of ICT facilities for staff and students.

It is also dependent upon staff and student training in the appropriate educational use of ICTs. It is now recognised that a specific set of skills (in addition to technical ones) is required by staff in order to successfully tutor students online and to facilitate online student discussion groups and assessments. Gilly Salmon's five stage model of e-moderating offers a combined approach for developing technical and learning skills in students through the use of online group activities (see Salmon 2002 and 2004). Chin 2004 provides an excellent introduction to using ICTs in HE. It highlights the benefits of ICTs in teaching and learning, and provides practical advice and real examples from a wide range of subject disciplines.

Part-time and Distance Learners and ICTs:
Concerns have been expressed, however, in relation to ICTs and equal opportunities.

One area relates to any gender differences in being comfortable with and having access to computers. The other concerns access to distance learning courses, where there is an increasing tendency to have learning materials launched as web pages rather than as paper-based materials, thus precluding participation by students without the necessary hardware and telecommunications links. In particular, there are worries that students in the more remote areas of some countries in Eastern Europe, Africa, and the Indian sub-continent for whom distance learning would greatly improve the accessibility of education would in fact be excluded if the emphasis was upon non-print-based materials. This would include the need for access to other media, such as video, as well as to computers.

However, issues of equity affect not only overseas students. Evidence suggests that some students in the UK may also have difficulty gaining access to ICTs in terms of computers and internet connections. Although there may be equal access for full-time on-campus students the availability of hardware off-campus is far from equal. Some part-time students have reported having difficulties obtaining access to a telephone, let alone email facilities. Similar difficulties are encountered by some distance learning students. Gender and socio-economic inequity has been reported in surveys of Open University students for many years. The study by Kirkup et al. in 1995 indicated that there were differences in domestic ownership of a variety of common ICTs (such as video, CD player and computer), 'with people in paid employment and those in higher occupational positions more likely to own such technology' (cited in Kirkup and von Prummer 1997 p. 55).

These differences could adversely affect access to the curriculum by the very people the Government is wanting to attract into HE via its widening participation agenda – those from the lower social classes.

6.1 Gender and ICTs

The women within each socio-economic group are less likely to own such equipment than are the men, 'and women at the lower end of the strata, such as single unemployed mothers, very rarely own any information technologies' (cited in Kirkup and von Prummer 1997 p. 55). Although more recent OU surveys indicate that access to some forms of ICTs increases year by year the gender differential remains. Even where there were ICTs within a household it was very often the males within the household who have the greater access to and control over the technology.

Kirkup 2001 reports that fewer women than men:

- have access to ICTS at home and work;
- use email for personal use, for study and for work;
- use computer conferencing at home.

In the latter case, nearly twice as many men as women use computer conferencing in their studies. Overall the gender gap in use of household-based media is greater than work-based, and the gender gap with the newest media (such as mobile technology) is greatest. However, women do not resist using ICTs, indeed women are happier than men to learn to use ICTs in the context of their subjects of study, but they do have to compete to gain access to those ICTs, especially at home. All of this can lead to women students being disadvantaged where a significant amount of studying or coursework requires the use of ICTs to complete them.

6.2 Disabled students and ICTs

One of the key areas that the Special Educational Needs and Disability Act 2001 (SENDA) has drawn attention to is the accessibility of electronic materials for disabled students.

The use of ICTs can substantially enhance the learning experience for some disabled students. There is great potential for learning and teaching in the new mobile technologies: Personal Digital Assistants (PDAs) can bring great benefit to disabled students. There are an increasing number of 'assistive technologies' available for Personal Computers, the provision of which can help ensure an equivalent learning experience for disabled students. Some computers with special auditory facilities or with large screens are available for the visually impaired, for instance. Adapted keyboards can be used by students with cerebral palsy. Other forms of low-tech ICTs, such as audio tapes or video tapes will clearly be unsuitable for some students. The difficulties experienced by dyslexic students have been greatly reduced with the advent of the spell checker and thesaurus built into word processors and of the predictive word processor and speech synthesis. The same programmes have also enhanced the learning of the hearing impaired students as have the various literacy software packages. There are many excellent sets of resources available on disability and the advantages and potential difficulties of the use of IT by disabled students.

Techdis (funded by JISC) is a major player in this area, and has produced or co-produced a number of excellent guides for HE practitioners. (See Becta and JISC TechDis Service 2003 and Phipps et al. 2002.) Another useful resource is in the form of Appendix 1 of GDN 2001d: 'Enabling Technology to Support Students with Dyslexia on Fieldwork', which provides a useful summary of suppliers of software, screen/text readers, spellcheckers, talking calculators, and so on. See also 'A guide to good practice for staff teaching d/Deaf students in art, design and communication' by Mole and Peacock 2002.

One of the main areas where accessibility is an issue is the format of web pages. Many screen readers cannot function correctly if the material is inappropriately formatted. The main standards to which university websites must comply are those provided by the W3C (World Wide Web Consortium), which has developed the Web Accessibility Initiative (**www.w3.org/WAI/**).

They provide detailed guidance about how to make websites accessible, and a memory prompt for concepts from the W3C Recommendation in the form of the following Quick Tips list* available from **www.w3.org/WAI/quicktips/**:

- **Images & animations.** Use the **alt** attribute to describe the function of each visual.
- **Image maps.** Use the client-side **map** and text for hotspots.
- **Multimedia.** Provide captioning and transcripts of audio, and descriptions of video.
- **Hypertext links.** Use text that makes sense when read out of context. For example, avoid "click here."
- **Page organization.** Use headings, lists, and consistent structure. Use **CSS** for layout and style where possible.
- **Graphs & charts.** Summarize or use the **longdesc** attribute.
- **Scripts, applets, & plug-ins.** Provide alternative content in case active features are inaccessible or unsupported.
- **Frames.** Use the **noframes** element and meaningful titles.
- **Tables.** Make line-by-line reading sensible. Summarize.
- **Check your work.** Validate. Use tools, checklist, and guidelines at **http://www.w3.org/TR/WCAG**

(* Copyright © 1998–2003 World Wide Web Consortium, (Massachusetts Institute of Technology, European Research Consortium for Informatics and Mathematics, Keio University). All Rights Reserved. Reproduced with permission under the terms of the W3C document license.)

Many of the current standards of accessibility for web pages assist all web users, not just disabled students, because they are a great deal clearer to navigate through and to read. The use of a Content Management System (CMS) by an institution will be of assistance in ensuring consistency in the quality of web materials. A CMS enables centralised web managers with significant technical expertise and decentralised web authors/editors with less technical expertise to create, edit, manage and publish all the content of a web page (such as text, graphics, video, and so on) in accordance with a given framework or set of standards. A CMS is a tool or set of tools that facilitates this process.

Task 11 Access to ICTs

Given the potential difficulties of some students (because of issues of inequity of access and ICTs or because a student is disabled) what alternatives do you need to consider when preparing your teaching and learning materials?

Commentary

It may be that because of economic considerations (particularly where there are large student numbers on a course) the teaching methods have to include a significant proportion of IT-based work. If this is the chosen route then the specific requirements for the course must be made very clear to students in the initial information issued about the course, and certainly before enrolment. IT facilities (and skills?) then become a pre-requisite for that course, or need to be provided at the start of the course.

You need to obtain information about how you can acquire materials in order to meet the needs of students who are disabled. For example: are there facilities at your institution to prepare materials in Braille for visually-impaired students, or on audio-tape for the dyslexic, blind or slightly hearing-impaired student? In addition, all web-based materials must meet the current accessibility standards.

Although more problematic and time-consuming for the tutors, it may be necessary to use dual or even multiple forms of teaching and communication methods in order to accommodate the limited resources of some students. For example: although there are many advantages for tutor and students in using email for communication (including tutorials) tutors may, in addition, have to offer telephone, fax, face-to-face, or even letter options for those part-time or distance-learning students without access to email facilities.

Section 7:

Assessment

7.1 Introduction

According to the joint report of the CRE, EOC, and CVCP 'Higher Education and Equality: a guide', (1997, p. 4), there are more student complaints about unfair assessment than in any other area. Research evidence indicates that differences in performance between racial and ethnic groups cannot be explained biologically, nor can gender differences be explained this way. It is much more likely that environmental or psycho-social factors can cause differences in performance. For instance, concern has been expressed at Cambridge and Oxford about the greater number of male candidates than women who are awarded first-class degrees, even though female students excel at A level. It has been suggested that 'Oxbridge examiners tend to reward bold, assertive essays – the typically male style – rather than the painstaking and cautious work more often produced by female undergraduates' and that a cautious style should not be valued less highly than a confident one (MacLeod 1998).

Bias by markers is another source of inequity, but anonymous marking can address this to a large extent, and there is concern about the actual content of tests. There is also growing interest in the evidence that the form in which the assessment takes place will affect the outcomes, with some students performing better with some forms of assessment than others. For instance, there is evidence that females do less well in timed examinations due to higher levels of anxiety (Gipps 1994, Chapter 9). This is a particularly crucial issue in relation to summative assessment. A variety of modes of assessment should therefore be considered. However, it is clear that some methods of assessment are far more time-consuming for hard-pressed academics to prepare and administer than are others.

Task 12

Which of the following do you think should be given the greater consideration when designing student assessments: the limited amount of time which tutors have to devote to the assessment of students; or the desire for students to achieve the highest possible mark for every assignment?

Commentary

No, this isn't a trick question, but it does seem to be one which isn't often asked by teachers. Of course, we are all working to tight schedules and with increasing numbers of students, but some consideration of student preferences should perhaps also come onto the agenda. As always the reality is likely to be something of a compromise. These issues (and many more) are explored in the excellent book by Morgan et al. 2004. Ryan 1997 emphasises the need for assessment criteria to be 'explicit and fair' (p. 5). A number of specific issues are explored below.

7.2 Content of tests

The test material itself can be one source of poor performance, for example because of the language used or because of the inadequate or stereotyped representation of some groups. The Fawcett Society 1987 examined a range of exam papers to look at the gender roles reflected in the papers. They analysed the 1986 school exam papers from the English and Welsh Examination Boards and identified seven types of discrimination:

1. The overall effect of a paper can be biased because reference is made predominately to one sex.
2. The presentation of men and women in the paper is stereotyped: men are admirable, women frivolous.

3. The questions are about subjects of interest only to boys.
4. The assumptions that people are male and so is the genotype, girls and feminine pronouns go into brackets if they appear at all.
5. The authors of texts studied are almost exclusively male.
6. Passages chosen for criticism and comment have a strong male bias.
7. An opportunity to mention eminent women has been missed.

Although it is to be hoped that things have improved considerably since 1986, it is worth using the above as a checklist against which to measure your assessments from time to time, considering the implications for race, ethnicity, religion or belief, dis/ability, age and sexuality as well as gender. It is just as relevant to higher education.

7.3 Multiple choice questions
There is a great deal of evidence to suggest that males do better with objective tests, that is multiple-choice questions (mcqs) than do females. Part of the explanation offered for this is that females will leave an answer blank rather than guess the answer. There is some suggestion that this relates to the lack of confidence by females (Gipps 1994, Chapter 8). In a study of 15 year olds by Murphy 1981, (cited in Gipps, p. 215) boys in particular expressed their anxiety about the free response mode of assessment which they considered to be more difficult, whereas the girls expressed a dislike of multiple-choice items because 'you don't have to think'. Careful consideration therefore needs to be given to the proportion of assessment (especially summative assessment) that is carried out using MCQs.

With the increasing use of software such as 'Questionmark Perception' being used to automate self-assessment tests for students, saving staff a great deal of time, there is a real concern that disabled students may be disadvantaged.

Care needs to be taken to ensure that software of this kind meets the accessibility standards referred to in Section 6.2 and that an appropriate amount of extra time is allowed for disabled students to complete such tests, especially when used for summative assessment.

7.4 Anonymous marking
The perceived gender of the student can have a powerful effect on the mark ascribed (Gipps 1994, p. 275). Anonymous marking would remove this bias and would also protect students from different ethnic groups. Much of the impetus for anonymous marking came from research at Cardiff University, where a far lower proportion of women than men gaining first and upper second degrees was reversed when anonymous marking was introduced (Wojtas 1993). Belsey 1988 also shows that women's degree classes improve when a system of anonymous marking is used.

Anonymous marking of coursework and exams is regarded as extremely important for lesbian, gay and bisexual (LGB) students in order to ensure that their work is not marked down because of their sexuality by any tutors with homophobic attitudes. It is regarded as equally important that students who choose to submit coursework involving discussion of LGB issues are not penalised because of their choice of topic.[vii]

The University of Leeds introduced anonymous marking in the 1999–2000 academic year for University examinations, but it stopped short of introducing it for all forms of assessment: 'It remains at the discretion of the School/Department whether or not this procedure is adopted for any other form of assessment (e.g. Departmental examinations, essays)' (University Assessment Handbook). In my view we will not be able to move towards eliminating bias in marking until all forms of assessment are submitted anonymously.

Consider:
Essays/exam papers by male students are consistently being marked more highly by the (mainly male) tutors in your department /institution – even though anonymous marking has been introduced. What action could be taken to address this issue?

7.5 'New' forms of assessment

Overseas students can experience difficulties with different kinds of assessment as used in the UK. Whereas they may previously have been rewarded for academic performance that drew heavily on the work of others (which is regarded in some cultures as a compliment to those whose work they copy), they may find themselves penalised for not being independent or critical, or even find themselves accused of plagiarism (Ryan 1997, pp. 19–20). Research undertaken by Kinnell 1990 and others with overseas students found that the students appeared to revere their tutors and often expected to receive all of their knowledge from them, rather than through independent study. They had a tendency to accept that knowledge unquestioningly (p. 64 and passim Chapters 2 and 3). Similarly some overseas students may have problems with group work, or with presentations, either because of lack of language skills or because of lack of self-confidence. UK students from minority ethnic groups can face similar problems, especially some women who, in some cultures, are encouraged to be self-effacing.

Ironically, although the research indicates a stated preference by women for more interactive work and shared learning, many mature women students sometimes experience difficulties in participating in assessed group work because of their commitments outside of the university. They often find that the organisational work falls to them, which only increases the burden of group work (Ryan 1997, p. 24).

If we are to take a flexible and inclusive approach to meeting the needs and preferences of our students we need to consider offering a combination of forms of assessment within a programme of study, and preferably within each module.

The number of types of assessments now available are huge, and although some are more appropriate than others for particularly subject disciplines it is still possible to offer a variety to each cohort of students. Books such as Brown et al. 1996 and Morgan et al. 2004 are invaluable in this area, and you may also be inspired by something in the list of assessment methods identified in the QAA Subject Benchmark statements, compiled by Judith Waterfield and Bob West, which can be found in 'Mapping the field of assessment methods' in SWANDS 2002, p. 95.

The use of IT in assessment (especially in formative assessment) can greatly reduce the workload of hard-pressed academic staff (particularly if you have large student groups) and can be a very positive way of introducing flexibility in terms of time, place and pace for students. However, as discussed earlier, the needs of disabled students must be carefully considered when introducing automated methods.

7.6 Written work

Consider:
Approximately 15% of students on one of your courses are studying in English as a second or third language. Should you be more lenient with those students with regard to penalising bad grammar and spelling when marking exam scripts?

Research indicates that there is inconsistency within institutions, and even from one academic to another within the same department, when it comes to penalising 'wrong' grammar or structure in students written work (Ryan 1997, p. 22). Unless there are explicit guidelines for academics it is difficult for the individual to know whether or not to penalise students with 'poor' English. Overseas students are of course the main ones for whom this is a potential source of grievance, although UK students for whom English is not their first language may also feel unfairly treated if marks are deducted for poor spelling or grammar, when they are not included specifically as assessment criteria.

Makepeace and Baxter 1990 in their study of overseas students found that language, in particular comprehension, was the most common explanation for academic failure. They suggest that extra, early remedial language tuition is needed for some students, but emphasise that 'more rigorous insistence on adequate language qualifications for all entrants may ensure that new entrants do not require remedial tuition' (p. 47). Brown 1994 looks in depth at the particular demands on students' language made by arts subjects. His work is primarily based on the experiences of postgraduate students of English literature and history from Japan, Korea and Taiwan. He suggests that effective writing in this subject discipline demands a control of English which is not easily acquired in a second language. Harris 1995 suggests that universities need to provide not only linguistic support for overseas students 'but a subject-sensitive marking frame which acknowledges cultural as well as linguistic differences and does not make the error of assuming that concept and grammar can be simply unyoked' (p. 89).

Task 13

It might be helpful to look again at the assessment criteria for the modules/courses on which you teach. Do they include reference to spelling and grammar? Can allowances be made for students for whom English is not their first language? Look, as well, at the learning outcomes for those modules/courses.

Commentary

Since assessment criteria should be linked to learning outcomes marks should neither be added nor deducted for spelling and/or grammar unless they are explicitly stated as learning outcomes. Of course, if either or both are so bad that the meaning is lost, then marks may well be deducted because other criteria are not met. If the standard of English is held as a sufficiently important concern for a particular course as to warrant its inclusion as a learning outcome then departments would need to consider offering remedial help for those students who persistently fell short of the required levels.

However, the number of students for whom this is necessary should be minimal if a pre-entry language requirement is specified.[viii]

To make allowances for some students (that is overseas or UK students from minority ethnic groups) would be a very contentious move and one which could rightly be challenged on grounds of injustice. In any case, this would be a retrograde step as regards the issue of anonymous marking.

Kinnell 1990 found that on the whole overseas students seemed positive about the task of essay and assignment writing, though some 'were anxious to have clear guidelines and much help with what they saw as a new activity or which varied from their previous educational experience'. Others welcomed essay writing as 'an opportunity to be free from the spoon-feeding they had previously experienced and as a chance to pursue their own interests' (pp. 52–3). The Institutional Racism in HE Project (2003) warns: 'Assessment of a student's language abilities should not influence assessment of other skills' (p. 90).

Disabled Students

Although some disabled students, through careful advanced planning, may cope well through most of the year without any extra help, they may request special facilities or allowances during timed written examinations. In order to be able to fully demonstrate their knowledge and competence they may require longer to complete the examination paper or need to use word processing facilities, or need to have a short break or breaks during the examination time due to lack of physical stamina. Although such arrangements might cause a few extra headaches for the examinations officer it is possible to overcome all of these problems.

Similarly appropriate arrangements may be needed for coursework assessments. In either case students may require an amanuensis or scribe – someone to write from dictation by the student. A detailed statement about a student's needs will be included in their assessment of study strategies and skills. In some instances the process of meeting those needs can become fairly complex, but support is usually available from an institution's disability services unit.

Dyslexic students

Although it is now generally accepted in the UK that dyslexic students are in need of understanding and, more importantly, extra support, dyslexic students can still experience great difficulties in following a course of study. In particular it is understandably very stressful for them when asked to produced large amounts of written work as this can affect other areas of their work as it is so demanding for them.

Task 14

If you do not already know, find out what support/services your university provides for dyslexic students. This information may well be available from the disability services unit or the student welfare or support office.

[vii] From: Liverpool University Guild Lesbian Gay and Bisexual Committee *Queering the campus ... some ideas for work in education.* Reproduced in Ryan (1997), Appendix 6, p. 225.

[viii] Leeds, in common with many other universities, requires overseas students to provide evidence of an adequate level of proficiency in English. The preferred test is IELTS (International English Language Testing System) since this is specifically designed to assess the use of English for academic purposes and is widely available. The TOEFL (Test of English as a Foreign Language) is also acceptable. However, whilst having a high reputation for its reliability, TOEFL does not always include tests of writing and speaking and these associated tests have to be requested specifically. Whichever test is used as evidence before admission to the University, the Language Centre tests all new international students whose first language is not English *after* they have registered with the University, in order to identify any students who may need language support during their academic course.

Section 8:

Conclusions

8.1 Attitudes can make all the difference

Sensitivity of staff and students needs to be high on the agenda if a supportive, non-oppressive environment is to be created and increasing diversity among staff and students is to be positively valued. In one study some mature students reported that a lack of understanding by tutors for their situation can be detrimental to their self-confidence, particularly for students already struggling to cope with the academic content of a course when returning to study after a break of some years. They also reported incidents of being humiliated by tutors because they don't possess some of the background knowledge which is part of, for instance, a contemporary 'A' level course. Women students reported that they were often not taken seriously in subject areas traditionally associated with men and that they sometimes felt intimidated by male lecturers who used autocratic teaching styles and responded negatively to their contributions (Ryan 1997, pp. 24 & 25).

Disabled students may often feel isolated. Some may have difficulty participating fully in the curriculum and in the social life because of lack of appropriate facilities. Where participation is possible, extra effort and a lot of forward planning is needed on the part of the student. Whilst disabled students clearly do not want to be patronised they will sometimes need extra help and understanding from both staff and students. Staff need to set an example in this and in particular they need to ensure that they are aware of the individual needs of particular disabled students in their groups. Gay and lesbian students are often the butt of jokes about sexuality and recipients of derogatory remarks made by other students. Staff need to challenge such behaviour in students.

Lack of sensitivity towards overseas students or to British students from minority cultural backgrounds is often due to lack of knowledge about those cultures.

Very often there are misunderstandings over verbal and non-verbal communication. Inappropriate language (because different students are not aware of each others social conventions) can create barriers. For example, the lack of the use of 'please' and 'thank you' by some students is not a deliberate attempt to be rude or blunt, but simply that the equivalent words just don't exist in some languages. Misunderstandings can also occur when brothers or members of close-knit groups based on ethnicity collaborate on the production of written work. This is based on the norm of fraternal help and contradiction of this practice by the tutor needs to be done with sensitivity.

Non-verbal communication can also be misinterpreted. Whereas in some cultures the use of eye contact is a sign of listening behaviour, in others the lack of eye-to-eye contact is a sign of respect for the person with whom they have contact (see Okorocha 1996.) Many students interviewed on the UKCOSA video spoke of how happy they are to speak to other students and the lecturers about their countries and cultures. Sadly, however, such students are sometimes not welcomed by others into their group for small group work. This clearly needs careful management by the tutor.

Although the differences between students is something to be celebrated, that very difference can lead to feelings of isolation for some students. [For more information about culture shock, loneliness and stress for overseas students see the following: Furnham and Bochner 1986; Persaud 1993a; and Persaud 1993b.] Often all that is needed is a friendly chat with another student or member of staff for an overseas student to feel less depressed. However, students from any culture can reach the stage of needing professional help should they become too depressed.

All staff need to be familiar with the various agencies available so that students can be referred to the appropriate one should problems arise. Sometimes the problem can be medical, at other times to do with accommodation, or with coursework.

Task 15

If you have not already done so, it is probably advisable to find out the names and phone numbers of the various professional agencies available for students, including the Counselling Service and Student Welfare Office within your institution. Some services may only be provided by the Students' Union at your institution.

Consider:
An Asian woman in one of your groups rarely makes a contribution during group discussions. You have also noticed her from time to time sitting on her own in the coffee bar. What action (if any) should you take?

The isolation suffered by women overseas students and UK women students from minority ethnic groups in some HEIs can be particularly acute. They may also experience sexism and sexual harassment as well as racism. Although now dated in many ways, the following book remains a classic in its field: Goldsmith and Shawcross 1985 'It ain't half sexist, Mum: women as overseas students in the UK'. Women academic staff may be the first people to whom women students turn. You need to know which groups exist within your university for women students, and in particular which structures are in place for putting overseas women students in touch with each other.

8.2 It can be done
Experience within many institutions indicates that it is possible to make equal opportunities an integral part of the curriculum rather than it being treated as an 'add-on'. 'It needs to be part of a general philosophical approach to all facets of learning and teaching' (Ryan 1997, p. 10). In other words a culture change is needed in all aspects of the life of an institution and it needs to be adopted by all staff and all students.

If the curriculum is known to be inclusive and the learning environment friendly and supportive to all students, this in turn will go a long way to attracting a more representative student body to an institution.

Although there are common themes and issues that have been highlighted during the research, it is clear that different solutions will suit individual lecturers and tutors, depending on their subject matter, their own teaching style, and the composition of their student population. There are no simple and easy answers, and solutions will usually only be found by working with students and issues at the particular time. What is most important is adopting a flexible and reflective approach, being aware of disadvantage suffered by some groups of students, and being prepared to respond to students' individual needs. (Ryan 1997, p.19)

We cannot, however, take **only** a reactive stance to these issues. Inclusivity also needs to be built into the design of the curriculum.

Task 16

To reflect on your practice overall in relation to equality, diversity and inclusivity, take a look at the checklist provided in Appendix 2. A positive response to the suggestions there reflects a positive attitude to these important issues and an imaginative approach to the curriculum, the result of which will mean an inclusive curriculum for all. Add other action points in the three blank rows in the table.

Commentary

Hopefully, by addressing the items included in the checklist for this final task, you will be able to bring together your thoughts and reactions to the issues raised by the whole of this guide. Whilst a great deal of thought still needs to be given to making the curriculum in HE a truly inclusive one, my hope is that the need for a guide such as this will diminish in the not too distant future, when the sorts of practices suggested here are embedded in the practice of all as a matter of course.

References

Aboutorabi, Mohsen (1995) 'International research students: problems and expectations.' *Journal of International Education* 6 (3), pp. 55–62.

Advisory, Conciliation and Arbitration Service (ACAS) (2003a) *Religion or Belief in the Workplace: a Guide for Employers and Employees.* ACAS. (**www.acas.org.uk/publications/pdf/guide_religionB.pdf**) [accessed 04 March 2004].

Advisory, Conciliation and Arbitration Service (ACAS) (2003b) *Sexual Orientation and the Workplace: a Guide for Employers and Employees.* ACAS. (**www.acas.org.uk/publications/pdf/guide_sexualO.pdf**) [accessed 26 April 2004].

Adams, M. (2000) *Changing the Culture: Addressing the Needs of Disabled Students.* Unpublished paper.

Anglia Polytechnic University (n.d.) *Assessing Policies, Practices and Procedures – Guidance for Managers* (**www.apu.ac.uk/equalops/rraa_guidance.doc**) [accessed 26 April 2004].

Ashcroft, Kate, et al. (1996) *Researching Into Equal Opportunities in Colleges and Universities.* London: Kogan Page.

Athena Project (2003a) *Athena Guide to Good Practice 1999 to 2002.* Athena Report 22. (**http://corp.etechb.co.uk/campaigns/athena/Athena/AthenaGoodPracticeGuide99-02new.pdf**) [accessed 26 April 2004].

Athena Project (2003b) *2003 Survey of Science Engineering and Technology in Higher Education (ASSET) Preliminary Report* [accessed 26 April 2004]. (**http://corp.etechb.co.uk/campaigns/athena/Athena/ASSETPrelimReportFinal.pdf**)

Becta and JISC TechDis Service (2003) *Inclusive Learning and Teaching: ILT and Disabled Learners.* A set of leaflets written by Simon Ball Chris Barber, Louise Buckel, Sal Cooke, Eddie Gulc, Judith Mole and Allan Sutherand. Becta and JISC TechDis Service.

Belsey, C. (1988) 'Marking by number.' *AUT Women* 15, pp. 1–2.

Borland, J. and James, S. (1999) 'The learning experience of students with disabilities in higher education. A case study in a UK university.' *Disability and Society* 14 (1), pp. 85–101.

Bowl, Marion (2003) *Non-Traditional Entrants to Higher Education: 'They Talk About People Like Me'* Stoke on Trent: Trentham Books.

Brown, Peter (1994) 'International arts students at British universities: great expectations and hard times.' *Journal of International Education* 5 (1), pp. 33–40.

Brown, Sally, Race, Phil and Smith, Brenda (1996) *500 Tips on Assessment.* London: Kogan Page.

Carter, J, Fenton, S & Modood, T (1999) *Ethnicity and Employment in Higher Education.* London: Policy Studies Institute. (Summary – **www.psi.org.uk/publications/ethnic/ethhefind.htm**) [accessed 26 April 2004].

Cattell, R.B. (1963) 'Theory of fluid and crystallized intelligence: a critical experiment.' *Journal of Educational Psychology* 54, pp. 1-22.

References

Child, Dennis (1993) *Psychology and the Teacher.* London: Cassell, 5th edn.

Chin, Paul (2004) *Using C&IT to Support Teaching.* London: RoutledgeFalmer.

Commission for Racial Equality (2002a) *Code of Practice on the Duty to Promote Race Equality.*

Commission for Racial Equality (2002b) *A Guide for Further and Higher Education Institutions.* (For details of how to obtain the Code and the Guide see: **www.cre.gov.uk/publs/cat_duty.html#code**) [accessed 26 April 2004].

Conefrey, Theresa (1997) 'Gender, culture and authority in a university life sciences laboratory.' *Discourse and Society* 8 (3), pp. 313–40.

Corlett, Sophie and Cooper, Deborah (1992) *Students with Disabilities in Higher Education: a Guide for All Staff.* Skill: National Bureau for Students with Disabilities.

Davie, Grace (1994) *Religion in Britain Since 1945: Believing Without Belonging.* Blackwell.

Department for Education and Skills (2002) *Providing Work Placements for Disabled Students: a Good Practice Guide for Further and Higher Education Institution.* (Ref: DfES/0024/2002) (**www.lifelonglearning.co.uk/placements/index.htm**) [accessed 26 April 2004].

Department for Education and Skills (2003a) *The Future of Higher Education.* Norwich: The Stationery Office Limited Cm 5735. (**www.dfes.gov.uk/hegateway/uploads/White%20Pape.pdf**) [accessed 26 April 2004].

Department for Education and Skills (2003b) *Widening Participation in Higher Education.* (**http://www.dfes.gov.uk/hegateway/uploads/EWParticipation.pdf**) [accessed 26 April 2004].

Department for Trade and Industry (DTI) (2003a) *Equality and Diversity: Age Matters.* (**www.dti.gov.uk/er/equality/age_consultation.pdf**) [accessed 26 April 2004].

Department for Trade and Industry (DTI) (2003b) *Explanatory notes for the Employment Equality (Sexual Orientation) Regulations 2003 and the Employment Equality (Religion or Belief) Regulations. 2003* (**www.dti.gov.uk/er/equality/so_rb_longexplan.pdf**) [accessed 26 April 2004].

Disability Rights Commission (2002a) *Code of Practice for the Elimination of Discrimination in the Field of Employment Against Disabled Persons or Persons Who Have Had a Disability.* (**www.drc-gb.org/thelaw/practice.asp**) [accessed 26 April 2004].

Disability Rights Commission (2002b) *Disability Discrimination Act 1995 Part 4 Code of Practice for providers of Post 16 education and related services.* (**www.drc-gb.org/thelaw/practice.asp**) [accessed 26 April 2004].

Disability Rights Commission (2003a) *Central Services and Facilities – Good Practice Guide.* DRC. (EDU 10) (**www.drc-gb.org/publicationsandreports/pubseducation.asp**) [accessed 26 April 2004].

Disability Rights Commission (2003b) *Examinations and Assessment Good Practice Guide.* DRC. (EDU 9) (**www.drc-gb.org/publicationsandreports/pubseducation.asp**) [accessed 26 April 2004].

Disability Rights Commission (2003c) *Learning and Teaching Good Practice Guide.* DRC. (EDU 12) (**www.drc-gb.org/publicationsandreports/pubseducation.asp**) [accessed 26 April 2004].

Disability Rights Commission (2003d) *Libraries and Learning Centres Good Practice Guide*. DRC. (EDU 14) (**www.drc-gb.org/publicationsandreports/pubseducation.asp**) [accessed 26 April 2004].

Disability Rights Commission (2003e) *Staff Development Good Practice Guide*. DRC. (EDU 13) (**www.drc-gb.org/publicationsandreports/pubseducation.asp**) [accessed 26 April 2004].

Doyle, Carol and Robson, Karen (2002) *Accessible Curricula: Good Practice for All*. University of Wales Institute, Cardiff. (**www.techdis.ac.uk/resource.html**).

ECU (2003a) *Dealing with Racism on Campus*. Equality Challenge Unit. (**www.ecu.ac.uk/updates/show.asp?Code=5**) [accessed 26 April 2004].

ECU (2003b) *Implementing the New Regulations AGAINST DISCRIMINATION Practical Guidance*. Equality Challenge Unit. (**www.ecu.ac.uk/publications/downloads/SO+RBguide.pdf**) [accessed 26 April 2004].

ECU and JNCHES(2003) *Partnership for Equality: Action for Higher Education*. Equality Challenge Unit and Joint Negotiating Committee for Higher Education Staff. (**www.ecu.ac.uk/publications/**) [accessed 26 April 2004].

Fawcett Society (1987) *Exams for the Boys*. Hemel Hempstead: The Fawcett Society.

Fraser, Kym (ed.) (due October 2004) *Education Development in the Higher Education Sector: Context, Structure, Processes and Strategies*. London: Taylor and Francis.

Fraser, Kym and Sanders, Ellen (forthcoming) *Educating University Teachers: Participation and Access Issues for Students Who Have a Disability* **in** Fraser, Kym (ed.) (forthcoming).

Furnham, A. and Bochner, S. (1986) *Culture Shock: Psychological Reactions to Unfamiliar Environments*. London: Methuen.

Geography Discipline Network (2001a) *Issues in Providing Learning Support for Disabled Students Undertaking Fieldwork and Related Activities*. Authors: Mick Healey, Alan Jenkins, Jonathan Leach and Carlyn Roberts. GDN at University of Gloucester.

Geography Discipline Network (2001b) *Providing Learning Support for Blind and Visually Impaired Students Undertaking Fieldwork and Related Activities*. Author: Ifan Shepherd. GDN at University of Gloucester.

Geography Discipline Network (2001c) *Providing Learning Support for d/Deaf and Hearing Impaired Students Undertaking Fieldwork and Related Activities*. Authors: Terry Wareham, Gordon Clark and Crissie Laugesen. GDN at University of Gloucester.

Geography Discipline Network (2001d) *Providing Learning Support for Students with Hidden Disabilities and Dyslexia Undertaking Fieldwork and Related Activities*. Authors: Brian Chalkley and Judith Waterfield. GDN at University of Gloucester.

Geography Discipline Network (2001e) *Providing Learning Support for Students with Mental Health Difficulties Undertaking Fieldwork and Related Activities*. Authors: Jacky Birnie and Annie Grant. GDN at University of Gloucester.

Geography Discipline Network (2001f) *Providing Learning Support for Students with Mobility Impairments Undertaking Fieldwork and Related Activities.* Authors: Vince Gardiner and Naseem Anwar. GDN at University of Gloucester.

(To view, print and download the above GDN guides see the website at: **www.glos.ac.uk/gdn/disabil/index.htm** and for details of how to purchase a hard copy set see the website at: **www.glos.ac.uk/gdn/disabil/dishard.htm**) [accessed 26 April 2004].

Gipps, Caroline (1994) *A Fair Test?: Assessment, Achievement and Equity* Buckingham: Open University.

Goldsmith, Jane and Shawcross, Valerie (1985) *It Ain't Half Sexist, Mum: Women as Overseas Students in the UK.* World University Service and UK Council for Overseas Student Affairs.

Goodwin, M.H. (1990) *He-said-she-said: Talk as Social Organization Among Black Children* Bloomington: Indiana University.

Gowers, Sir Ernest (1986) *The Complete Plain Words.* Edited by Sidney Greenbaum and Janet Whitcut. HMSO (originally published in 1954).

Grant, C.A. (ed.) (1992) *Research and Multicultural Education: From the Margins to the Mainstream* London: Falmer Press.

Grewal, Ini, Joy, Sarah, Lewis, Jane, Swales, Kirby and Woodfield, Kandy (2002) *'Disabled for Life?': Attitudes Towards, and Experiences of, Disability in Britain.* National Centre for Social Research on behalf of the Department for Work and Pensions. London: Department for Work and Pensions (Research Report 173). (**www.dwp.gov.uk/asd/asd5/rrep173.asp**) [accessed 26 April 2004].

Gumperz, J.J. (ed.) (1992) *Language and Social Identity.* Cambridge: Cambridge University Press.

Hall, Stuart (1992) 'The West and the Rest: Discourse and Power' in *Formations of Modernity,* Cambridge: Open University Press, pp. 275–320.

Harris, Robert (1995) 'Overseas students in the United Kingdom university system.' *Higher Education* 29, pp. 77–92.

Higher Education and Equality: a Guide (1997) Report prepared by Janet Powney, Sheila Hamilton and Gaby Weiner and published jointly by the Equal Opportunities Commission, the Commission for Racial Equality, and the Committee of Vice-Chancellors and Principals of the Universities of the UK, June.

Higher Education Funding Council for England (2003a) *Funding for Widening Participation in Higher Education: Responses to Consultation and Funding for 2003-04 to 2005-06.* HEFCE. (**www.hefce.ac.uk/pubs/hefce/2003/03 14.htm**) [accessed 26 April 2004].

Higher Education Funding Council for England (2003b) *HEFCE Strategic Plan 2003–08.* HEFCE. (**www.hefce.ac.uk/Pubs/hefce/2003/03 35.htm**) [accessed 26 April 2004].

Higher Education Funding Council for England (2003c) *Implementing HR Strategies: a Guide to Good Practice.* HEFCE (**www.hefce.ac.uk/pubs/hefce/2003/03%5F37/default.asp**) [accessed 26 April 2004].

References

Higher Education Funding Council for England, Universities UK, Standing Conference of Principals: Teaching Quality Enhancement Committee (2003) *Final Report of the TQEC on the Future Needs and Support for Quality Enhancement of Learning and Teaching in Higher Education.* (**www.hefce.ac.uk/Learning/TQEC/**) [accessed 26 April 2004].

HESA (2002-03) (**www.hesa.ac.uk/**).

HM Land Registry (2002?) *Cultural Diversity: a Resource Booklet on Religious and Cultural Observance, Belief, Language and Naming Systems.* London: HM Land Registry. (**www.diversity-whatworks.gov.uk/documents/HMLandRegistryCulturalDiversity.pdf**) [accessed 26 April 2004].

HMSO (Her Majesty's Stationery Office) Website **www.legislation.hmso.gov.uk/legislation/uk.htm**) The site includes the full text of all legislation enacted by the UK Parliament. [accessed 26 April 2004].

Holdsworth, Angela (1988) *Out of the Dolls House: the Story of Women in the Twentieth Century.* London: BBC Books.

Horn, J.L. (1967) 'Intelligence – why it grows, why it declines.' *Trans-action* 5, pp. 23-31.

HUCS (Heads of the University Counselling Services) (1999) Degrees of Disturbance: The New Agenda (The impact of increasing levels of psychological disturbance amongst students in higher education). Published by *The British Association of Counselling.* (**www.hucs.org**) [accessed 26 April 2004].

Independent Review of Higher Education Pay and Conditions (Bett Committee) (1999) London: Stationery Office. (Summary of recommendations – **www.archive.official-documents.co.uk/document/irhec/irhec.htm**) [accessed 26 April 2004].

Institutional Racism in Higher Education Project *(2003) University of Leeds Case Study Executive Summary and Final Report.* A research project funded by the Department for Education and Skills. Research undertaken by Ian Law, Debbie Phillips and Laura Turney (Centre for Ethnicity and Racism Studies) at the University of Leeds.

James, Deborah and Drakich, Janice (1993) *Understanding Gender Differences in Amount of Talk: a Critical Review of Research.* In Tannen (1993), pp. 281–312.

James, D.E. and Dovaston, V.M. (1991) *Adult Participation in Universities.* Guildford: University of Surrey.

Jenkins, Alan (2003) *Virtually Interesting Fieldwork.* Oxford Brookes Teaching Forum (**www.brookes.ac.uk/virtual/NewTF/48/tf_48jenkins.htm**) [accessed 26 April 2004].

Johnston, Chris (2004) 'Women accepted in record numbers.' *The Times Higher* January 30, p. 10.

Kinnell, Margaret (ed.) (1990) *The Learning Experiences of Overseas Students.* Milton Keynes: Society for Research into Higher Education & Open University Press.

Kirkup, Gill (2001) *Gender, Computer-mediated Learning, and the Student Experience.* (A presentation to the University of Lund (Sweden) in May 2001 at a special seminar on gender and ICTs in the university.) (**http://kn.open.ac.uk/public/document.cfm?docid=1326**) [accessed March 2004].

References

Kirkup, Gill and von Prummer, Christine (1997) 'Distance education for European women: the threats and opportunities of new educational forms and media.' *European Journal of Women's Studies* 4, pp. 39–62.

Law, Ian, Phillips, Deborah and Turney, Laura (2004) *Institutional Racism in Higher Education*. Stoke on Trent: Trentham Press.

Learning and Skills Council (2003a) *Equality and Diversity Guidance: Guidance on the Sexual Orientation and Religion or Belief Regulations 2003*. LSC. December 2003 (Ref: MISC/0937/03 03) (**www.lsc.gov.uk**) [accessed 26 April 2004].

Learning and Skills Council (2003b) *Successful Participation for All: Widening Adult Participation Strategy* LSC March 2003 (Ref: LSC/0606/03) (**www.lsc.gov.uk**) [accessed 26 April 2004].

Lewis, Vicky and Habeshaw, Sue (1990) *53 Interesting Ways to Promote Equal Opportunities in Education*. Bristol: Technical and Educational Services Ltd.

MacLeod, Donald (1998) 'Confidence trick.' *Guardian Higher*, Tuesday 13 January.

Macpherson of Cluny, Sir William (1999) *The Stephen Lawrence Inquiry*. London: Stationery Office. (**www.archive.official-documents.co.uk/document/cm42/4262/4262.htm**) [accessed 26 April 2004].

Makepeace, Eira and Baxter, Arthur (1990) 'Overseas students and examination failure: a national study.' *Journal of International Education* 1 (1), pp. 36–48.

Maltz, D.N and Borker, R.A. (1982) *A Cultural Approach to Male-female Miscommunication*. In Gumperz (1992), pp. 196–216.

Miller, Casey and Swift, Kate (1995) *The Handbook of Non-sexist Writing for Writers, Editors and Speakers*. Women's Press, 3rd edn.

MindOUT for Mental Health (2003) *Line Managers' Resource: a Practical Guide to Managing and Supporting Mental Health in the Workplace*. MindOUT Project.

Mole, Judith and Peacock, Diane (2002) *Learning, Teaching and Assessment: a Guide to Good Practice for Staff Teaching d/Deaf Students in Art, Design and Communication*. University of Wolverhampton.

Molloy, Donna, Knight, Tim and Woodfield, Kandy (2003) *Diversity in Disability: Exploring the Interactions Between Disability, Ethnicity, Age, Gender and Sexuality*. London: Department for Work and Pensions (Research Report 188) (**www.dwp.gov.uk/asd/asd5/rports2003-2004/rport188/Inside.pdf**) [accessed 26 April 2004].

Molloy, Donna, Knight, Tim and Woodfield, Kandy (2004) *Diversity in Disability: Exploring the Interactions Between Disability, Ethnicity, Age, Gender and Sexuality*. London: Department for Work and Pensions (Research Summary of Report 188) (**www.dwp.gov.uk/asd/asd5/summ2003-2004/188summ.pdf**).

Morgan, Chris, Dunn, Lee, Parry, Sharon and O'Reilly, Meg (2004) *The Student Assessment Handbook: New Directions in Traditional and Online Assessment*. London: RoutledgeFalmer.

References

Murphy, P. (1981) *An Investigation into Mode of Assessment and Performance for Girls and Boys.* Paper presented at the British Educational Research Conference, Manchester, September.

NATFHE (2002) *Discrimination on the Grounds of Religion or Belief: a Discussion Document* (**www.natfhe.org.uk/down/religion.pdf**) [accessed 26 April 2004].

The National Committee of Inquiry into Higher Education (Dearing Committee) (1997) London: Stationery Office. (**www.leeds.ac.uk/educol/ncihe**) [accessed 26 April 2004].

Okorocha, Eunice I. (1996) 'Some cultural and communications issues in working with international students.' *Journal of International Education* 7 (2), pp. 31–8.

Office for National Statistics (2003) *Census, April 2001.* (**www.statistics.gov.uk**) [accessed March 2004).

Parker, Viv (1999) 'Thinking about disability access to HE.' *New Academic* 8 (2) Summer, pp. 19–21.

Persaud, Rajendra (1993a) 'The loneliness of the long distance student.' *Journal of International Education* 4 (2), pp. 45-51.

Persaud, Rajendra (1993b) 'Stress and the sojourning student.' *Journal of International Education* 4 (1), pp. 27-37.

Phipps, Lawrie, Sutherland, Allan and Seale, Jane (eds.) (2002) *Access All Areas: Disability, Technology and Learning.* JISC TechDis Service and ALT.

Quality Assurance Agency for Higher Education (the QAA) (1999) *Code of Practice for the Assurance of Academic Quality and Standards in Higher Education Section 3: Students with Disabilities.* QAA. (**www.qaa.ac.uk/public/cop/copswd/contents.htm**) [accessed 26 April 2004].

RCPsych (Royal College of Psychiatrists) (2003) *The Mental Health of Students in Higher Education.* Council Report CR112. (**www.rcpsych.ac.uk/publications/cr/cr112.htm**) [accessed 26 April 2004].

Rich, Adrienne (1986) *Blood, Bread, and Poetry: Selected Prose 1979-1985.* London: Virago.

Ryan, Janette (1997) *Equal Opportunities in the Curriculum. Good Practice Guide.* Equal Opportunities Action Group, Oxford Brookes University.

Salmon, Gilly (2002) *E-tivities: the key to active online learning* London: RoutledgeFalmer.

Salmon, Gilly (2004) *E-moderating: the key to teaching and learning online* London: RoutledgeFalmer.

Sanders, Claire (2004) Rise in disabled grant uptake *The Times Higher* January 30, p. 10.

Skill: National Bureau for Students with Disabilities (1997) *The Coordinator's Handbook.* Skill [Includes 12 pages of details of organisations from whom advice can be obtained, and a list of useful publications.]

Skill: National Bureau for Students with Disabilities (2002) *A Guide to the DDA for Institutions of Further and Higher Education.* Skill 5th edn.

Skill: National Bureau for Students with Disabilities (2003a) Press release 08.04.2003 Response to 'Widening Participation in Higher Education' published in April 2003 (**www.skill.org.uk/press/archives/08042003.asp**) [accessed 26 April 2004].

Skill: National Bureau for Students with Disabilities (2003b) *Disability Discrimination Post-16 Education: The 5 Step Test.* Skill (**www.skill.org.uk/info/infosheets/dd_5step.doc**) [accessed 26 April 2004].

Spencer, Sarah and Fredman, Sandra (2003) *Age Equality Comes of Age.* London: IPPR.

Stonewall (2004a) *Discrimination at Work is So Over – Employees Briefing.* Stonewall (**www.stonewall.org.uk**) [accessed 26 April 2004].

Stonewall (2004b) *The Employment Equality (Sexual Orientation) Regulations Guidelines for Employers.* Stonewall (**www.stonewall.org.uk**) [accessed 26 April 2004].

SWANDS (South West Academic Network for Disability Support) (2002) *SENDA Compliance in Higher Education: an Audit and Guidance Tool for Accessible Practice Within the Framework of Teaching and Learning.* Edited and written by Judith Waterfield and Bob West. A HEFCE funded Project: Improving Provision for Disabled Students 1999-2002. Co-ordinated by the University of Plymouth. (**www.plymouth.ac.uk/assets/SWA/Sendadoc.pdf**) [accessed 26 April 2004].

Swartz, E. (1992) *Multicultural Education from a Compensatory to a Scholarly Foundation.* In Grant (1992), pp. 32–46.

Tannen, Deborah (1993) *Gender and Conversational Interaction.* Oxford: Oxford University Press.

Turney, Laura, Law, Ian and Phillips, Debbie (2002) *Institutional Racism in Higher Education Building the Anti-racist HEI: a Toolkit.* Centre for Ethnicity and Racism Studies, University of Leeds. (**www.leeds.ac.uk/cers/toolkit/toolkit.htm**) [accessed 26 April 2004].

UKCOSA (1994) *Partners in Discovery: Developing Cultural Awareness and Sensitivity.* Video: 30 minutes. UK Council for Overseas Student Affairs.

Universities and Colleges Employers Association (2000) *Equal Opportunities in Employment in Higher Education: a Framework for Partnership.* UCEA.

University College Worcester (n.d.) *QAA Code of Practice – Students With Disabilities Departmental/ Service Profiling Tool* (**www.worc.ac.uk/services/equalopps/Proftool.doc**) [accessed 26 April 2004].

University College Worcester (2004) *Strategies for Creating Inclusive Programmes of Study* (SCIPS) Pilot Project (**http://scips.worc.ac.uk**) [accessed 26 April 2004].

University of Leeds (2004a) *Ahead-4-Health* – a unique website that allows students to think about mental health in a personal and interactive way. Screen savers on PCs across campus advertise the site at times of peak student stress, such as Freshers Week and exams. The site has had an average of 30,000 hits per month from both on and off campus. Future plans include more interactivity and on-line self-help. (**www.leeds.ac.uk/ahead4health**) [accessed March 2004].

University of Leeds (2004b) *Helping Students with Mental Health Difficulties.* 2nd edn. (**www.leeds.ac.uk/uscs**) [accessed March 2004].

Weller, Paul (1992) 'Religion and equal opportunities in higher education.' *Journal of International Education* 3 (3), pp. 53–64.

Wojtas, Olga (1993) 'Anonymous marking at Edinburgh.' *Times Higher Education Supplement* 16 April, p. 2.

Wright, Sue and Lander, Denis (2003) 'Collaborative group interactions of students from two ethnic backgrounds.' *Higher Education Research and Development,* 22 (3) November, pp. 237–52.

Yorkshire and Humber Assembly (2004) *Religious Literacy: a Practical Guide to the Region's Faith Communities.* 3rd edn. (Available from Y and HA, email: **mary.white@yorkshirechurches.org.uk**).

Resources

General
Cabinet Office - What works? website is a tool for sharing best practice across the civil and wider public service. It showcases some creative ideas used by the public, private and voluntary sector to address the advancement of equal opportunities and diversity in the quest for cultural change. (**www.diversity-whatworks.gov.uk**) [accessed 26 April 2004].

Becta
British Educational Communications and Technology Agency (Becta) (formerly the National Council for Educational Technology) is the Government's lead agency for ICT in education (www.becta.org.uk/) [accessed 26 April 2004] **Ferl** is the Becta advice and guidance service supporting individuals and organisations in making effective use of ILT within the Post Compulsory Education sector. It offers numerous individual resource items which can be viewed or downloaded from the Ferl resource banks at **http://ferl.becta.org.uk/** [accessed 26 April 2004].

Gender
The Athena Project aims to promote the advancement of women in science engineering and technology in higher education and a significant increase in the number of women recruited to the top posts. (**www.etechb.co.uk/campaigns/athena.asp**) [accessed 26 April 2004].

AWiSE the UK **Association for Women in Science and Engineering** is an organisation set up to support women in the field of Science Engineering and Technology. (**www.awise.org**) [accessed 26 April 2004].

The Equal Opportunities Commission (EOC) is the leading agency working to eliminate sex discrimination in 21st Century Britain. (**www.eoc.org.uk**) [accessed 26 April 2004].

The Fawcett Society is a national organisation, working to create a greater equality for women in Britain and for change on issues at the heart of women's daily experience. (**www.fawcettsociety.org.uk**) [accessed 26 April 2004].

Race
Commission for Racial Equality (CRE)
The CRE is a publicly funded, non-governmental body set up under the Race Relations Act 1976 to tackle racial discrimination and promote racial equality. (**www.cre.gov.uk**) [accessed 26 April 2004].

Channel 4. Black and Asian History map

A gateway to websites about black and Asian history across the British Isles. (**www.blackhistorymap.com**) [accessed 26 April 2004].

Institute of Race Relations (IRR)

The IRR is at the cutting edge of the research and analysis that informs the struggle for racial justice in Britain and internationally. (**www.homebeats.co.uk**) [accessed 26 April 2004].

Runnymede Trust

Runnymede is the foremost UK-based independent think tank on ethnicity and cultural diversity. Its core mandate has been to challenge racial discrimination, to influence anti-racist legislation and to promote a successful multi-ethnic Britain. (**www.runnymedetrust.org**) [accessed 26 April 2004].

Culture and Religion or Belief

SHAP - The Working Party on World Religions in Education. Producers of the SHAP calendar and many other useful resources. (**www.shap.org/**) [accessed 26 April 2004].

International Students

UKCOSA (UK Council for Overseas Student Affairs) now called The Council for International Education is an organisation for international students, offering information and advice. Suppliers of: 'Partners in discovery: developing cultural awareness and sensitivity' video. Contact: email: **enquiries@ukcosa.org.uk** (**www.ukcosa.org.uk/**) [accessed 26 April 2004].

Sexual orientation

Stonewall For Lesbian and Gay Equality. Parliamentary lobbying is Stonewall's core activity. Research, training, information provision and building alliances is given focus and resources. (**www.stonewall.org.uk**) [accessed 26 April 2004].

Lesbian and Gay Employment Rights (LAGER) is an independent organisation here to help lesbians and gay men who are experiencing problems at work or whilst looking for work. (**www.lager.dircon.co.uk**) [accessed 26 April 2004, but may be closing down if funding not found].

Disability
Association of Disabled Professionals (ADP)

The Association of Disabled Professionals exists to provide a forum to enable disabled people share personal experience of successful professional development, and help create conditions for other disabled people to realise their career and workplace ambitions. (**www.adp.org.uk**) [accessed 26 April 2004].

BBC website - a perspective on disability

The BBC's website that reflects life as a disabled person. (**www.bbc.co.uk/ouch**) [accessed 26 April 2004].

The Department for Work and Pensions Disability Unit

The DWP has the lead on disability issues within Government. (**www.disability.gov.uk/**) [accessed 26 April 2004].

Employers' Forum on Disability

The Employers' Forum on Disability is the employers' organisation focused on the issue of disability in the workplace. (**www.employers-forum.co.uk/www/index.htm**) [accessed 26 April 2004].

The Disability Rights Commission (DRC)

The DRC is an independent body, established by Act of Parliament in 2000 to eliminate discrimination against disabled people and promote equality of opportunity. In 2003 it launched its *Educating for Equality: HE Campaigns Pack* to raise awareness of the new rights and duties within HEIs (see DRC 2003a – 2003e for some of the booklets included). They are distributed by ECU and include advice on *Learning and Teaching, Examinations and Assessment* and *Libraries and Learning Centres.* (**www.drc-gb.org**) [accessed 26 April 2004].

National Association of Disablement Information on Advice Services (DIAL UK).

The site has a wide range of information for disabled people and their carers in the UK. DIAL groups are set up by people with experience of disability and provide a free, impartial and confidential service of information and advice in local areas. (**www.crossd17.freeserve.co.uk/dial%20uk.htm**) [accessed 26 April 2004].

The National Disability Council

This site helps people to find out about their civil rights. The site is managed by the Disability Unit in the Department for Work and Pensions. (**www.disability.gov.uk/**) [accessed 26 April 2004].

The National Disability Team (NDT)

'The NDT is contracted by the Higher Education Funding Council for England (HEFCE) and the Department for Employment and Learning for Northern Ireland (DELNI) to undertake the service of a national team to improve provision for disabled students in higher education.' The NDT provides support for HEFCE/DELNI funded projects. The projects focus on two main areas of activity: to improve provision in small and/or specialist institutions that currently have little provision for, or experience in supporting, students with disabilities; and to develop and disseminate resources relating to the learning and teaching of disabled students. These projects are expected to have a sector-wide impact. (**www.natdisteam.ac.uk/**) [accessed 26 April 2004].

Skill: the National Bureau for Students with Disabilities

Skill is 'a national charity promoting opportunities for young people and adults with any kind of disability in post-16 education, training and employment across the UK'. It published its *Guide to the DDA for institutions of further and higher education* in 2002. This was followed in 2003 by its *Disability Discrimination Post-16 Education: The 5 Step Test* (2003b) as an aid to assessing whether disability discrimination has taken place in respect of further and higher education. The 1997 Coordinator's Handbook also remains a very useful resource. (**www.skill.org.uk/**) [accessed 26 April 2004].

Royal National Institute for the Blind (RNIB)

The RNIB campaigns at a national level to influence government policy and bring about lasting change for people with sight problems. It also funds research into preventing and treating eye disease and promotes eye health by running public health awareness campaigns. The RNIB also provides services such as braille, talking books and computer training, which focus on the needs of people with sight problems. It also produces the 'See it right' pack –12 booklets that offer practical advice on planning, designing and producing information that is accessible to everyone. Ranging from producing large print and Braille, to accessible websites and clear print guidelines. (**www.rnib.org.uk**) [accessed 26 April 2004].

British Deaf Association (BDA)

The BDA is 'the largest national organisation run by Deaf people, for Deaf people. The British Deaf Association wants to see a society where deaf people have full and unrestricted access to all walks of life thus becoming equal citizens, contributing and participating freely.' (**www.britishdeafassociation.org.uk**) [accessed 26 April 2004].

RNID for deaf and hard of hearing people

RNID is the largest charity representing the 8.7 million deaf and hard of hearing people in the UK.

Its role includes funding research, campaigning and lobbying to change laws and government policies and raising awareness about hearing loss through information, training and consultancy. It offers communication services and equipment, and helps deaf people into employment. (**www.rnid.org.uk/index.htm**) [accessed 26 April 2004].

British Dyslexia Association (BDA)

The BDA is 'the voice of dyslexic people'. They 'offer advice, information and help to families, professionals and dyslexic individuals. [They] are working to raise awareness and understanding of dyslexia, and to effect change'. They produce the 'Dyslexia Style Guide' and the 'Study Skills and Technology' guide (**www.bda-dyslexia.org.uk**) [accessed 26 April 2004].

Mind

The Mental Health Charity. Mind is the leading mental health charity in England and Wales, and works for a better life for everyone with experience of mental distress. (**www.mind.org.uk**) [accessed 26 April 2004].

National Institute for Mental Health in England

This NHS organisation works with others to 'improve services and support for people who experience mental distress'. (www.nimhe.org.uk/index.asp) [accessed 26 April 2004].

Terence Higgins Trust (THT)

The THT is the leading HIV & AIDS charity in the UK and the largest in Europe. THT delivers health promotion campaigns and direct services from offices across the UK to people with or affected by HIV and people at risk. (**www.tht.org.uk**) [accessed 26 April 2004].

Age

Civil Service Cabinet Office diversity website: Age Diversity website provides civil servants – employees, managers, and HR people - with a central point of information on all aspects of the diversity agenda. (**www.diversity-whatworks.gov.uk/age/background.asp**) [accessed 26 April 2004].

Employers' Forum on Age (EFA) is a network of employers confronting age discrimination in the workplace. Its role is to remove barriers to achieving an age-balanced workforce by influencing key decision makers, supporting organisation members and informing all employers of the benefits of a mixed-age workforce. (**www.efa.org.uk**) [accessed 26 April 2004].

Appendix 1:

Learning Cycle/ Styles/ Preferences/ Approaches[ix]

The Experiential Learning Cycle

Learning is a continual process and it is **not** a passive process. We remember 10% of all we hear, 50% of all we see and 90% of all we do. The figures seem to vary in different versions of this brief maxim, but the message is always the same: we learn best by doing, by experience. Good learning materials will encourage active learning.

Neither does learning happen in straight lines, that is it is not just a simple process of going through a few stages from beginning to end and finishing, and *hey presto* the learning is complete. Rather it has been likened to a cycle or a spiral by various people. Kolb combined these two concepts of experiential learning and cyclical learning in his four-stage Experiential Learning Cycle (Kolb 1984). The cycle moves through 'active experimentation', 'concrete experience', 'reflective observation' and 'abstract conceptualization' (page 42). This cycle has been adapted many times by many people. My own interpretation of it, which I have found to be useful in a higher education setting, is shown below.

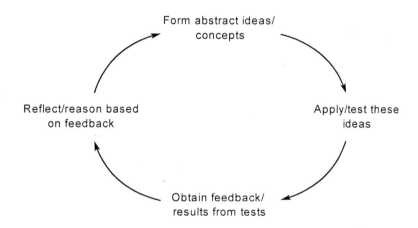

Loosely adapted from: Kolb, D.A. (1984) Experiential Learning: Experience as the Source of Learning and Development. Prentice Hall.

Learning styles: Honey and Mumford Learning Styles Questionnaire

All students have preferences about **how** they learn. There are several alternatives to analysing this. One is the Honey and Mumford Learning Styles Questionnaire and the four learning styles the authors have identified: **activist, reflector, theorist** and **pragmatist**. Their analysis is loosely based on Kolb's learning cycle. They suggest that the four styles of learning are associated with particular stages in the learning cycle. If, for example, your preferred style is that of activist, you are more likely to feel comfortable at Kolb's stage of 'concrete experience'. In practice, most people show a preference for at least two of the styles. However, since the aim is to complete the full learning cycle it follows that we should also aim to develop all four styles of learning if we are to fully benefit from all aspects of learning. The Learning Styles Questionnaire and how to score it is available in Honey and Mumford (1992). It is also available **for a fee** on Peter Honey's website: **www.peterhoney.com/main/**

Honey, Peter and Mumford, Alan (1992) The Manual of Learning Styles, 3rd edn. Maidenhead, Berkshire: Peter Honey.

Honey, Peter and Mumford, Alan (1995) Using Your Learning Styles, 3rd edn. Maidenhead, Berkshire: Peter Honey.

Learning preferences: Holist and Serialist

These two approaches characterise ways in which learners deal with new topics (uncertainty). The **holist** prefers a framework - a big picture - of the topic, and then fills in the details. A **serialist** copes better with a step-by-step approach to the topic. Students can operate in both ways (versatile) but will show preferences.

Type	Characteristics
Holist	<ul><li>Global learner</li><li>Seeks an overall picture</li><li>See relationships</li><li>Intuitive "jumps"</li><li>Asks where are they going and how will they get there</li></ul>
Serialist	<ul><li>Step-by-step approach</li><li>Aided by rules, algorithms</li><li>Follow procedures</li><li>Unaware of why or how</li></ul>

Pask, G. Styles & Strategies of Learning. *British Journal of Educational Psychology*, vol. 46, 1976, pp. 128–48.

Learning preferences: VARK

The VARK questionnaire developed by Neil D. Fleming, New Zealand and Charles C. Bonwell, USA, enables students to discover (or confirm) their learning preferences.

VARK	Characteristics of Preferences
V = Visual Graphic	Charts, Maps, Graphs, Pictures, Diagrams, Drawings, Flow charts, Videos, Use of colours, Picturesque Language, Spatial arrangement of items, Clever use of fonts, Brochures
A = Aural/Auditory	Talking, Speaking, Listening, Hearing, Debating, Discussing, Arguments, Phone Calls, Tapes, Clever use of speech, Story Telling, Meetings, Sayings, Discussion Groups, Poetry Reading
R = Read/Write	Lists, Dictionaries, Minutes, Handouts, Clever use of words, Interesting use of words, Correct use of words, Print, Quotations, Definitions, Contracts, Reports
K = Kinesthetic	Use all senses, Like examples, Applications, Models, Metaphor, Analogy, Role plays, Demonstrations, Trial and error, Field days, Tours, Hands-on, Experience, Testing, Trying
MM = Multimodal	Uses a balanced combination of the above

A website has been developed from where it is possible to take the VARK questionnaire interactively: **www.vark-learn.com**.

From the website you can also buy copies of Fleming, Neil D. and Bonwell, Charles C. (2001) *How Do I Learn Best? A Student's Guide to Improved Learning.* New Zealand.

Approaches to Learning
Students often have different intentions when they approach their learning.

Approach	Characteristics
1. Surface	• Focus on elements of content • Aim to remember as much as possible • Try to learn it off-by-heart
2. Deep	• Focus on content as a whole • Try to see the connections • Think about the structure as a whole • Try to understand the meaning
3. Strategic	• Intention to obtain the highest grade • Well organised study methods • Competitive

Entwistle, N. and Ramsden, P. (1983) *Understanding Student Learning.* London: Croom Helm. (Approach 3).

Marton, F. and Saljö, R. (1976) On qualitative differences in learning: I – outcome and process. *British Journal of Educational Psychology*, 46: 4–11. (For approaches 1 and 2).

[ix] This Appendix is based on materials written originally by Chris Butcher, Staff and Departmental Development Unit, and Joanna Brown, Learning Development Unit, University of Leeds.

Appendix 2:

Checklist for Good Practice

Equality, diversity & inclusivity in the curriculum	I do this	I need to consider this
1. Regularly review curriculum issues including race, gender, religion or belief, sexual orientation, disability and age		
2. Periodically assess the relevance to contemporary society of course materials		
3. Periodically assess the appropriateness of the modes and methods of delivery of the curriculum, in its widest sense		
4. Consider, in terms of coursework, resources, and so on, how people and places are represented and whether or not they are stereotyped		
5. Value the diversity included in the student body		
6. Assess and revise your teaching methods periodically		
7. Consider what are the most appropriate methods, timing and formats of assessment for the students you teach		
8. Assess whether the materials you provide for your students in both print and web format meet the current accessibility standards for disabled students		
9. Consider what to do if any colleagues or students use inappropriate language with respect to those who are disabled or hold religious beliefs or use language which is sexist, homophobic or ageist		
10.		
11.		
12.		

[The idea for this checklist came from those created by Clara Davies in the Staff and Departmental Development Unit at the University of Leeds, and from those included in 'The Anti-racist HEI: a Toolkit' by Laura Turney, Ian Law, and Debbie Phillips, University of Leeds.]